MAGICAL FASHIONISTA

Dress for the Life You Want

Tess Whitehurst is an intuitive counselor, energy worker, feng shui consultant, speaker, and author of *Magical Housekeeping*, *The Good Energy Book*, *The Art of Bliss*, and *The Magic of Flowers*. Her message is that we are completely empowered to heal ourselves and others, to live bravely, and to create the life of our dreams. She lives in Venice, California. Visit Tess online at www.tesswhitehurst.com.

Tess Whitehurst

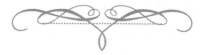

MAGICAL
FASHIONISTA

*Dress for the Life
You Want*

Llewellyn Publications
Woodbury, Minnesota

FIRST EDITION
First Printing, 2013

Book design by Rebecca Zins
Cover design by Ellen Lawson
Cover illustration by Mayumin/Japan Publicity Inc.
Interior backgrounds: Manga Patterns by Crazy Kira
(http://crazykira-resources.deviantart.com/art/
Patterns-36-149418100); Whitewashed Grunge Patterns and
Grungy Floral Patterns by WebTreats (http://webtreats.mysitemyway
.com/tileable-whitewashed-grunge-textures/ and http://webtreatsetc
.deviantart.com/art/Grungy-Floral-Patterns-124528488)
Llewellyn is a registered trademark of Llewellyn Worldwide Ltd.

Library of Congress Cataloging-in-Publication Data
Whitehurst, Tess, 1977–
Magical fashionista : dress for the life you want / Tess Whitehurst.
—First edition.
pages   cm
Includes bibliographical references.
ISBN 978-0-7387-3834-5
1. Fashion. 2. Clothing and dress. 3. Fashion—Psychological aspects.
4. Clothing and dress—Psychological aspects. 5. Self-actualization
(Psychology) 6. Positive psychology. I. Title.
TT507.W448 2013
746.9'2—dc23
2013022275

Llewellyn Publications
A Division of Llewellyn Worldwide Ltd.
2143 Wooddale Drive
Woodbury, MN 55125-2989

www.llewellyn.com

Printed in the United States of America

contents

3: You Are
an Interplay of Elements • 45

4: You Are
Exactly Where You're Supposed to Be • 71

5: You Are
a Celebration • 85

6: You Are
a Magician • 105

7: You Are
a Guru • 145

8: You Are
Ador(n)able • 177

9: You Are
Divine • 203

10: You Are
Pure Inspiration • 229

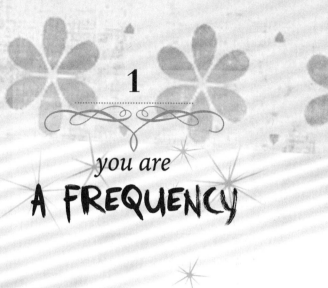

1

you are
A FREQUENCY

For a long time I thought fashion was fluff. Even though I enjoyed shopping for and wearing things I felt great in, I also felt like I was indulging in something of a guilty pleasure. I wasn't fully aware of it at the time, but perhaps my inner dialogue went something like this: "With all these *real* challenges in the world, who has time for fashion?"

And looking back, this is strange, because my career choices and the topics of my books and articles were all centered around the idea that our outer and inner environments are linked—and that even something as seemingly mundane as cleaning your house or painting your bathroom can have very positive repercussions in every area of your life. So why did clothes seem like a totally functional thing at best— maybe a little bit fun every now and then, but mostly a hassle or an impulsive splurge, and certainly nothing to really spend any *real* energy or attention on?

> In each
> of us resides a
> deep desire to be seen.
> We long for our beauty
> to be expressed in such
> a way that others will
> glimpse our essence.
> JENNIFER ROBIN, AUTHOR,
> ARTIST, AND FASHION
> CONSULTANT

The answer is multi-faceted. First, having judged fashion as superficial, I shoved the whole topic to the back of my consciousness and didn't even notice that I was doing it. Second—and more importantly from a self-growth perspective—having experienced a certain degree of what might be called neglect as a child, my attitude toward dressing, adorning, and caring for myself was something of a carryover from these early experiences. After all, until we consciously change the pattern, we're likely to treat ourselves the same way we were treated as children. And so I was not attuned with how joyful and treasured it would help me feel to reverently select and wear clothes that I loved. As you can imagine, for someone like me—who has made self-healing into a hobby—this was a victorious discovery and provided plenty of grist for the mill.

Perhaps the first inkling that my perspective on fashion could use some revisiting was when I saw the documentary *Bill Cunningham New York*. Momentarily glimpsing the world through the passionate eyes of veteran street fashion photographer Bill Cunningham helped me to realize that—while the whole fashion "thing" might appear superficial to anyone, say, camping out in the offices of *Vogue* magazine—it is actually a very personal art form. It's an interface between each of us and the rest of the world. It's a vehicle of self-expression and an aspect of lovingly observing and appreciating the people around us. And it's a way to celebrate the moment—to bring magic to the day. Considering that everything is connected, including everyone's mood and state of mind, these are certainly no small matters.

Once I began to see this way, I could reflect on my life and see the power of fashion at work: the times when I felt great about myself and had fun with my life, my wardrobe reflected that. The times when I felt ashamed or lacked confidence, my wardrobe reflected that, too. Was my mood a reflection of my wardrobe, or was my wardrobe a reflection of my mood? The answer, quite obviously, was both.

Every culture—from every time period, in every country on earth—has exhibited some sort of fashion-conscious behavior: it appears to be a characteristic of humans to take clothing and self-care choices beyond the realm of pure function. On the personal level, there is simply no denying that we feel better on a good hair or outfit day. And when we feel better, we make better choices, exude more confidence, and elicit a greater degree of respect from others. Really, why should we judge ourselves for this, and why should we—subtly or overtly—devalue this aspect of the human experience? A desire to express and enhance ourselves through our fashion choices is obviously human nature. We may as well berate ourselves for wanting to fall in love or walk barefoot in the grass.

To me, dismissing fashion as silly or unimportant seems like a denial of history and frequently a show of sexism—as if something that's traditionally a concern of women isn't valid as a field of academic inquiry.

TIM GUNN, AUTHOR, FASHION EXPERT, AND TV STAR

Consider the Lilies

Even though my dad's not especially religious, he *is* literary, and Luke 12:27 has always been his favorite Bible verse: "Consider the lilies, how they grow: they toil not, they spin not; and yet I say unto you that Solomon in all his glory was not arrayed like one of these." I know because he often reminded us of the fact as he recited it to my brother and me when we were kids. At the time, I thought it meant "Who cares what you wear or what job you have? Flowers are prettier than kings." But now I interpret it with a bit more depth. Now when I "consider the lilies," I consider how each and every blossom is a precious and divinely perfect being, exactly as it is—just as I am, just as you are, and just as Solomon was. His kingly raiment didn't hold a candle to his intrinsic beauty and perfection: he was not *arrayed* like one of these—he *was* like one of these.

And when it comes to fashion, we must start with this knowing. We are already beautiful! We already possess an innate divinity and glory. We are already lilies. Once we're grounded in this awareness, when we choose the royal vestments with which to array ourselves, we'll remember to experience joy (rather than worry or stress) as we do so, and to honor the perfect beauty that we already possess. We don't want to obscure this beauty; we want to allow it to shine.

Besides, let's be real: as lovely as the lilies are, if we tried to follow their example and go naked, in most cases it wouldn't go over too well. Indeed, one can only imagine that it wouldn't have worked out too well for Solomon.

What It Means to Be
a Magical Fashionista

Okay, now that we've debunked the myth of superficiality and really considered the lilies on a deep level, let's talk about what it means to be a magical fashionista.

If the universe is pure vibration—as many modern physicists and spiritual teachers have hypothesized that it is—you are both part of this vibration and a unique frequency unto yourself. According to metaphysical theory, the clearer and more appealing your transmission, the more positive attention and desirable conditions you will attract. And, like your radio station's loyal listener base, things that are in alignment with your vibration—i.e., conditions and people that are similar in essence to what you are broadcasting—will be irresistibly, magnetically drawn to you.

One of the most potent tools we have at our disposal to clarify and enhance our energetic frequency (and subsequently attract the things we want) is in our closet: our clothes and how we wear them. Few "inanimate" objects have more power over us (I use quotation marks here because nothing is truly inanimate when you consider that everything is alive with energy). To illustrate, consider that a single outfit can affect our moods and actions in ways that might reap such immediate blessings as getting the job, hooking a new love interest, or simply having a great day. And, since most of us wear *something* every single day, the power of a wardrobe—like flowing water softening the edges of a river rock—is relentless. Being a magical fashionista is about tapping into this power, fine-tuning our frequency, and turning up the volume on our personal radio station so that we can broadcast the messages we want to send, feel our best, and consistently attract the conditions we desire.

You have a divinely beautiful essence that is unlike any other. Like a diamond, a snowflake, or a cloud (or a lily! Or a king!), there has never been a being exactly like you, and there never will be. And while you are much too magical and mysterious to ever be nailed down or understood completely by anyone (including you), doing your very best to follow Shakespeare's advice to "know thyself" is a primary key when it comes to enhancing your personal vibration through the power of your wardrobe.

Once you begin to identify the beauty of who you are, how you feel, and how you naturally express your distinctive personal essence, you can adorn yourself with clothes and accessories that are specifically chosen to enhance your mojo and fuel your energetic momentum. That's why, throughout this book, we'll be exploring the unique inner and outer ways your essence expresses itself. Concurrently, we'll be looking at strategies—both practical and mystical—that will nourish and amplify that essence in the most attractive and beneficial of ways.

Your Unique Essence: Making First Contact

Grab a notebook or journal and, without thinking too much, reply to the following:

1. If I could be any animal, I would be a:

2. Three qualities I admire about this animal:

3. Three people I really admire (may include celebrities, family members, friends, fictional characters, or anyone else):

4. Three people I am (at least a little bit) jealous of:

5. Three dead celebrities I wish I could have hung out with:

6. Three qualities I would like to embody:

7. Three cities I would like to visit or move to:

8. Three qualities I wish people would use to describe me (even if I don't necessarily embody them now):

9. If I were a flower, I would be a:

10. Three qualities I admire about this flower:

Now take a moment to review what you've just written. Keeping in mind that your responses in some way reflect or indicate your inner essence, does your outer expression reflect this? For example, if you said that you want to visit India, do you ever listen to Indian music, watch Bollywood movies, or wear bangles? Or if you're jealous of Angelina Jolie, do you have at least one sleek black dress? (Often jealousy disappears when we claim the parts of our personality that the object of the jealousy represents.) If you wish you could have hung out with Jack Kerouac, do you sometimes have conversations about poetry, listen to Charlie Parker, or stay in a little cabin by yourself in the middle of nowhere? If you relate to lilacs, does your wardrobe, garden, or perfume reflect this?

When our inner and outer realities match, our goals become clearer, we manifest our desires more easily, life becomes amplified, and everything becomes a lot more fun. And since what we wear is literally sitting on the border between our inner and outer realities, our fashion choices are a really powerful way to get them in alignment.

The Power of Costumes

When I was fresh out of high school, instead of going to a normal college, I went to an acting school. And while I am no longer an aspiring movie star, I still value a lot of the wisdom I gleaned from my time there. Case in point: the power of costumes. I truly couldn't count the number of times I would be watching fellow students doing a scene over and over, and one day one of them would bring in a particular costume piece such as a hat or a scarf or a pair of shoes— and then suddenly the essence of the character would arrive in the room. The actor would no longer be plodding along through the lines but be alive with a magnetic and mesmerizing sort of confidence or authenticity or whatever it was the character called for. "Bravo," the teacher would say as the class cheered. "That hat really changed your whole attitude. You weren't acting anymore, you were *being*. We suddenly all believed you."

I know that in our day-to-day lives we are not acting, but we *are* being. And if we want to feel confident (or authentic or whatever), a particular scarf (or hat or pair of high heels) might be just the thing to help us get there. This is not a way of being phony or shallow: while the wardrobe addition might be "just a thing," our resulting feeling is more than that. Feelings powerfully underscore and influence our entire life experience, including our actions and how others see us and relate to us, and there is nothing phony about that.

So grab your journal again and jot down ten feelings you'd like to experience on a regular basis or qualities you'd like to possess. Then take a moment to think about "costume pieces" that might help you access these feelings or qualities. Cowboy boots? Luxurious pajamas? Bright red lipstick? Perhaps some of the items you're envisioning are already in your wardrobe, perhaps not. At this point, all I'm asking you to do is consider. We're still just getting warmed up.

Dress for the Life You Want

It is no mystery why one of the most recognizable and over-used clichés in the English language is "dress for success." Certainly most of us would agree that we do not expect to meet the love of our life or get our "big break" when we are wearing sweats and look like we just rolled out of bed. In my work as a feng shui consultant, this is similar to the precept "create the space for what you want to experience"—create a romantic atmosphere if you want to experience romance, create a serene study space if you want to experience scho-lastic success, and so on. It's really simple, and yet it can be helpful to remind ourselves that if we want to draw a certain condition into our life, it naturally increases our chances if we are actually prepared for it to occur. Additionally, if we can make preparing for it a fun exercise in joyful expectation, then all the better. It's a way of putting ourselves smack into the middle of the feeling we want to experience, which (if you will recall) tunes us to the frequency of our desire.

To put this another way: when we truly feel from the bottom of our hearts that we are destined for a particular life condition, and when we behave as if we already are the person who is experiencing that destiny, it becomes exponentially more likely that it will manifest in the physical realm. Again and again, we hear of famously successful people who have put this precept into action: Dale Carnegie, Russell Simmons, Louise Hay, Jim Carrey, and Oprah Winfrey, to name just a few. And of course dressing the part is a vital component—not to mention a fun one!

Grab that journal again, and respond to these questions:

- What do I want to experience in my career?

- How would I like to creatively express myself?

- What do I want to experience in my love life?

- What type of recognition and success do I crave?

- What does my ideal financial situation look like?

Now consider: do your clothes help you feel as if these conditions are already in place in your life? If not, or if you could use a little fine-tuning in this area, keep these goals in mind as you read through the remainder of the book, and be sure to jot down any ideas or sudden bolts of inspiration you may have.

Please note: if your most burning desire is (let's say) to go to more cocktail parties, I am not suggesting that you should wear a cocktail dress on an afternoon outing to your local coffeehouse. Since situation-appropriate attire usually looks and feels the best, you might instead choose to dress in a casual-yet-polished, coffeehouse-appropriate way that also makes you feel like someone *who is invited to* a lot of cocktail parties.

But then again, maybe you'll find yourself in the mood to look sexy, so you'll throw on heels for a trip to the supermarket, like my cousin and bestie, musician Emily Whitehurst. She recalls:

> *One time I decided (on a whim) to dress up to go grocery shopping at Trader Joe's in the middle of the day. I wanted to put on heels and a cute dress—something I would wear to go out at night or to play a show. My usual is jeans and a T-shirt, and I felt like being sexier that day for some reason. It totally worked! People were definitely looking at me differently, and I imagined they must have been wondering what I was up to since I was wearing that outfit grocery shopping. It was a fun way to use my own image for my entertainment.*

What Message Are You Sending?

There is also the matter of the messages we are sending out into the world via what we wear. While at first glance this might also seem shallow (after all, it's what's on the inside that counts, right?), it's actually not. Responding emotionally to the patterns that we see in the physical world is sim-

> As I
> continue to
> step more and
> more onto my path
> as a present-day priestess,
> dressing the part—wearing flowy,
> goddess-like clothes and jewelry, for
> example—helps amplify that intention.
> SEDONA SOULFIRE, SACRED DANCER AND PRIESTESS

ply an aspect of human nature. We all do it. In fact, as I alluded to above, in every culture on earth and in all time periods, particular types of clothing have sent particular types of messages to other humans regarding things such as one's personality, marital status, or degree of affluence. So instead of judging this or fighting against it, why not have fun with it and use it to our advantage?

For example, it may sound hackneyed, but it's real: have you ever really considered how much joy something as simple as a smile can create? You smile warmly at someone, which brightens her day, so she turns around and smiles warmly at three other people, which brightens *their* days, and so on. Now consider how much more you feel like smiling when you feel beautiful. In your mind's eye, see yourself feeling beautiful, smiling, and radiating the message that life is good and all is well. Everywhere you go, peace and beauty follow in your footsteps, creating ripples of peace and beauty in the very fabric of existence via the perceptions and emotions of your fellow humans, who spread the feelings to other humans, who spread the feeling to other humans, and so on and so on.

On the other hand, consider that you may be inadvertently sending the message via your wardrobe and according mood that you are "nothing special." Perhaps at some point you got the idea that shining your light too brightly was conceited or that wearing too lovely of an outfit meant that you were superficial. How sad for the world that they're missing out on those waves of peace and beauty! And how sad for you that others may not be as inclined to notice your brilliant spirit and all the amazing gifts you have to offer.

Of course, there are other highly specific messages we may potentially be sending with our wardrobe choices, such as "I value you and am pleased to be spending time with you," "I am worthy of respect," "I am really desperate for attention," or "I don't care about this stupid event."

So let's do another journal exercise. Number one to five and, without thinking too much about it, write down five messages you think you may possibly be conveying with your current wardrobe choices. (If you're feeling really brave, you might also ask an honest yet supportive friend.) Then, number one to five one more time and write down five messages that you would *like* to be sending with your wardrobe choices.

Notice What Colors, Patterns, and Textures You Crave

Are there certain colors or textures that you notice yourself drawn to again and again? Maybe a motif or pattern consistently catches your fancy, such as a feather print, paisley, or plaid. All these types of cravings can be your consciousness naturally wanting to absorb a particular quality of energy. If you wrap your waist in a feather-print scarf, for example, perhaps you feel light and fun, and this energy nourishes or balances you in exactly the way you most need to be nourished or balanced on a particular day. It's great to notice and honor these types of cravings. (Later, we'll talk more about consciously employing things like colors and patterns in order to boost or balance your mood.)

On the other hand, you want to be sure that you're not simply going on autopilot. Our tastes and preferences—not to mention current trends—are constantly in flux, so we must be awake to this and take this into account when choosing what to keep, what to get rid of, and what new items to bring into our wardrobes. What I mean is, if everyone knows to get you pink accessories or sweaters for Christmas because you've always loved pink, make sure you take a moment every now and then to assess whether or not this is still actually the case.

Your Personal Essence Playlist

Shamans and mystics of all varieties have incorporated music into their healing practices since time immemorial. Consider that in cinema (our most modern incarnation of shamanic storytelling), music can turn an otherwise flat scene into a hilarious scene or a terrifying scene or a scene that makes everyone cry. To begin to get more familiar with your essence and to smooth the transition to a harmonious synchronization of your inner and outer realities, I'd like you to create a personal-essence playlist. You might add to it and change it throughout your reading of this book, but let's start here:

Create a playlist for yourself containing at least eight (but possibly twelve or more) songs that embody the qualities, energies, and conditions you described in the previous journaling exercises. If you're feeling like you're not totally sold on those qualities or energies yet, that's okay. Just start somewhere—perhaps just look for songs that "click" for you and help you feel empowered and brave. Then, as you progress through your magical fashion journey, you can begin to notice what does and does not resonate with you and your essence, and shift your playlist accordingly.

You may find it helpful to get a little wild and go outside your usual music comfort zone. The first journaling exercise may have revealed that you want to travel to France. Take a little time and find some French music that has the vibe that you associate with visiting France, whether that calls for classical, jazz, electronic, pop, rap, or something else entirely. Or if you see that you're jealous of a celebrity that you also sort of can't stand, what qualities does that celebrity embody? Even if they're qualities you think you despise—such as "preening" and "self-absorbed"—maybe you can find a couple of catchy tunes that capture those qualities in a somehow pleasing way. (As I mentioned above, when something rubs us the wrong way, it is often an aspect of our own personality that we have not fully explored or accepted.)

Free association is okay, too. For example, you're not exceptionally likely to find a really great song about a camellia, but if you let yourself act from an artsy place rather than a logical one, you are likely to find a song that reminds you of the feeling it gives you to gaze at one. Additionally, in the subsequent exercises, you may have discovered that you want to embody more confidence, manifest a new job working with children, and send a message of joyful exuberance. See if you can find a song that inspires that confident strut you're craving, as well as a song that reminds you of the youthful innocence of children, plus a joyfully exuberant tune. Don't overthink it—there is no right or wrong, as long as you find songs that you intuitively feel resonate with the qualities and conditions you described. And again, you can always fine-tune your playlist later, so just do your best and start somewhere.

If you've ever seen the Isaac Mizrahi documentary *Unzipped*, you might remember that while he was designing his Mary Tyler Moore–inspired clothing line, he kept singing and humming the theme song to her TV show. Then, later, a remix of the song played during the fashion show. This exercise is similar, only while you may not be creating a line of internationally acclaimed couture, you're doing something even better: you're uncovering and spiraling more deeply into your own personal essence and finding your most joyful stylistic expression while simultaneously learning to enhance the quality and conditions of your life.

Now, once you've created your playlist, humor me for a few minutes, will you? When no one else is around, choose at least two songs and dance to them. (Or get even crazier and let the universe choose by pressing "shuffle.") Be silly and have fun. Turn up the music, relax, and let your body move however it wants to move. In the spirit of play, let yourself begin to embody the qualities in the music. Dancing is a very powerful exercise for getting your energy moving, liberating trapped energy, and getting us in touch with our true selves. Even if it seems like nothing is happening, believe me: this exercise will very quickly and ideally open you up to positive change and clear the way for the work ahead. Feel free to repeat it as desired. It will also be beneficial to listen to your playlist at convenient times throughout your normal routine: in your car, while you're cleaning house, and so on.

Clear Closet Clutter

Are you ready to really get your fashion energy moving and clear the decks for the fun and scintillating work ahead? Yes? Good! Let's approach the closet. But first, grab yourself a really big bottle or glass of water, light a stick of incense or diffuse a few drops of delicious-smelling essential oil, and put that playlist on the stereo…see, aren't we already having so much fun? Now pull everything out of your closet and your dresser—everything. Go ahead, pull it *all* out! Drape it over your bed if you need to, or strew it across the floor. Get every last little thing out of the corners. I know it's labor intensive, but it will really unstick your energy and get things flowing.

Since—as I've already mentioned several times—our inner and outer environments are linked, please drink a lot of water during this exercise to help purify your body and emotions right along with your wardrobe.

Now that you've done this, take a look at each thing individually. Does it fit the essence you want to emit, the qualities you'd like to possess, the conditions you'd like to manifest, and the messages you want to send? Do you love it? Does it fit you perfectly right now? Have you worn it within the last year (or if it was buried so deeply that you forgot it was there, are you excited about wearing it soon)? If it needs to be repaired, are you willing to repair it within the next seven days? Does it make you feel wonderful and attractive? If you answer no to any of these questions, you guessed it: it's time to get rid of it. Otherwise, you can place it back in your closet or dresser. (As a side note, you might want to take this opportunity to strategically streamline the way your wardrobe is organized.)

Although I prefer the pull-everything-then-put-the-good-stuff-back-in method, it's inspiring to note that author, fashion expert, and TV star Tim Gunn suggests making four piles when clearing closet clutter: the "soul-stirring pile," "the repair pile," "the giveaway pile," and "the throw-out pile." About the soul-stirring pile (which I think is a brilliant name, by the way), he emphasizes, "Keep in mind that this pile is not just for fantastic items; that flattering cotton tank you love goes in this pile too." Because truly: if it doesn't stir your soul (or at the very least potentially con-tribute to soul-stirring outfits, such as a perfect pair of black tights or a flawlessly fitting bra), why would you want to keep it around?

At this stage, you might find that you have a lot of stuff that you obviously want to get rid of, or you might not. You might realize that you have a ton of stuff you love, or you might only have a few pieces left hanging. Regardless, this process will help you get familiar with what you've got while giving you an opportunity to organize your things in a way that is convenient for examining and playing with your wardrobe (both of which you will be doing a lot of).

Let me emphasize that this is just an initial shift—a way to get rid of the most obvious extras in order to prepare for the creative, transformational work ahead. As you continue reading this book, it's very likely you'll suddenly realize that you're ready to get rid of a particular piece (or several). Or you might even want to repeat this process: pull everything out, examine it, and put it back in—again.

Just remember that from a divine and mystical perspec-tive, energy and resources are never lost—and that what you send out always comes back to you. So if you donate clothes that no longer fit you or that you no longer love (or never did), what are you sending out? Perfect "new" clothes (for someone else) and/or financial support (for the charity to which you donate). This means that you will not only be creating the space in your closet for a more beloved and functional wardrobe, you will also be racking up seri-ous karmic points in the clothing and finance departments.

Think of everything in terms of energy, and you will see that releasing things that you no longer value—and giving them to someone who will value them—always reaps generous rewards.

The Green Coat

I once had the most perfect green coat. It was velour grass green with a faux fur collar and cuffs: totally me. Then, alas, I left it on an airplane and never was able to retrieve it. Being a feng shui consultant and clutter-clearing enthusiast, I told myself over and over that— since nature abhors a vacuum (a clutter-clearing principle) and nothing is lost in Divine Mind (a metaphysical law)—I was destined for an equally wonderful coat that would miraculously present itself to me in perfect and divine timing.

Well, it didn't show and it didn't show. Finally, I realized that I had not fully released the original coat. Because I still actively regretted having left the coat on the plane, and because I still thought of it often as "my coat," in the realm of energy (which is all there truly is), the coat was still mine. Because it was in my energy field, it was impossible for the metaphysical laws cited above to work. In other words, according to the energetic patterns I was sending out, the coat was still taking up space in my life.

Once I realized this, I did a visualization in which I released the coat fully to the light while simultaneously affirming my trust that a new one would appear. Sure enough, within a week, I discovered a different—yet equally magical—green coat at a thrift store near my house.

The moral of the green coat? When you release old things—whether you lose them or donate them—fully release them: not only on the physical plane, but on the energetic plane as well. That way, new energy and resources will more easily and generously flow into your experience.

2

you are

A WORK OF ART

My father met my mother while she was getting her bachelor's degree in visual art. At the time, she was a classmate with his sister, who was one day to be my aunt. In many ways, growing up around both of these women taught me to look at the world through the eyes of an artist. Whether it is a painting, a photograph, or the sky at night, my eye naturally seeks the subtlest yet most vital shades of color, as well as things like proportion, texture, contrast, and flow. But what I value the most is how my primary female role models taught me how to look with the heart: to use the visual as a window into the ephemeral and to feel the emotional messages behind the things I saw in the physical world.

This chapter is about looking at yourself through the eyes of an artist. This will empower you to assemble outfits

> You are always
> congruent and you
> always look beautiful.
> If something doesn't look
> right, it's the outfit that doesn't
> really live up to your beauty,
> not the other way around.
>
> JENNIFER BUTLER, AUTHOR
> AND FASHION EXPERT

that highlight your unique, spectacular radiance. In the process, you will be dazzled by your own beauty, which will further inspire you to shine.

You Are a Natural Setting

A good place to begin is by looking at yourself as a landscape. Perhaps put on something neutral and look at yourself in the mirror. Remembering that you are exactly perfect as you are right now (just like any divine creature), take a look at things like your coloring, the quality of your hair and skin, your posture or bearing, and the shine of your eyes. Lovingly and with acceptance, look very deeply into your eyes to notice the hidden shades or dimensions there. Look for the undertones of your skin: are they olive, golden, cool, or pink? Even take a look at the blue, green, or purple shade of your veins in your hands and wrists. Also see if you can go beyond logical analysis to get a feeling for the energy that you are emitting. Then consider: if you were a natural landscape, where would you be? For example, you may be:

- a field of flowers surrounded by grass that has turned golden in the sun

- an aqua blue ocean lapping at fine white sand

- a forest of cedars

- rolling sand dunes in the desert

- a rocky cliff in the snow

- sunshine glittering on an alpine lake

- an underwater kelp forest

- the Grand Canyon at dawn

- a tropical rainforest

- the full moon over a lush meadow on a warm summer night

- black river rocks and white-water rapids under a cool blue sky

Just as it wouldn't make sense to judge a particular landscape as inherently better or worse than any other, you mustn't use this as an opportunity to judge or criticize yourself. Simply begin to get in touch with the unique quality of beauty that you possess.

Since it can be challenging to be objective about our own appearance, you may find it helpful to ask a trusted and truly supportive loved one for his or her opinion on what natural landscape you might resemble. (Then just take this into consideration—don't necessarily take it as gospel.)

Once you've discovered a landscape that feels right, you might like to take a moment to find some photos of this type of landscape online or in magazines. If you feel inspired, you could store the photos online or put them in your journal or scrapbook.

Now when you choose clothes, consider whether they complement the landscape that is you or whether they feel foreign to this landscape. One way I like to do this is by imagining that I'm choosing place settings and décor for a party that I am throwing in this landscape. If you were throwing a party in a forest of cedars, would you decorate with seashells and a bouquet of yellow tulips? Probably not. You might instead go for pine cones and tuberose. (Please note that this isn't about following any prescribed set of rules but about what *feels* right.)

When I first did this exercise, I noticed that I sometimes dressed myself like I was an aqua-blue tropical ocean or an English countryside in spring, when really I'm more like a California meadow in late summer or early fall. I realized why I never exactly felt ravishing in the floral, icy-and-jewel-toned sundress that I thought was so adorable on the hanger. I also realized why I did feel great in outfits that incorporated deeper colors like black and chocolate brown, along with colors that were more congruent with a golden, late summer–type setting, such as dusty or rosy pinks, burgundy or garnet reds, golden tones, and cream.

I even gained some insight into why I felt so much more like myself when I stopped dying my hair black and instead had it lightened to a more golden shade, a color that's reminiscent not only of my childhood end-of-summer hair color but also of a late summer hillside almost anywhere in California. It all fits together: I was born in California right at the end of summer, and fall is my favorite season. I found my groove.

Contrast

Jennifer Butler's brilliant book *Reinventing Your Style* introduced me to the concept of looking at one's own degree of visual contrast, just as a painter would look at a painting to determine what type of frame would best showcase its essence. Once you notice the extremes of color and how they appear in your personal makeup, you can mirror them with your wardrobe choices. This way, you won't overpower your beauty or detract from its drama, but you will complement it and allow it to retain its own perfect balance.

So let's go to the mirror again. In your personal coloring, other than your pupil, what is the darkest dark color that appears? And other than your teeth and the whites of your eyes (unless your hair and skin are both a deep chocolate brown—see below), what is the lightest?

If, for example:

- your hair is black and your skin is alabaster, your degree of contrast is high

- your eyes are brown, your skin is light, and your hair is red, your degree of contrast is medium

- your eyes are medium blue and your hair is light brown, your degree of contrast is medium

- your hair, skin, and eyes are light brown, your degree of contrast is low

- your hair, skin, and eyes are all very pale, your degree of contrast is low

- your hair, skin, and eyes are all deep chocolate brown and your teeth and the whites of your eyes are very white, your degree of contrast is high (according to Jennifer Butler, this is the only color combination that requires you to look at the whites of your eyes and teeth)

The goal, however, is not to determine whether you are high, medium, or low, but just to get a visual picture and feeling for your degree of contrast. Then you can assemble outfits in colors that are complementary to you (which you can determine using the principles in the previous "You Are a Natural Setting" section), with a similar degree of contrast. So, to illustrate, let's say that your degree of contrast is high: a high-contrast outfit such as something containing both black and white or both chocolate brown and buttercream would be a match contrast-wise. Or if your degree of contrast is medium, you could go with two colors in the medium range that contrast each other to a medium degree, such as lilac and royal blue or rose pink and toasty brown. If you're a low-contrast person, you could wear colors in your range that contrast each other to a subtle degree: buttercream and beige if your complexion is light, or olive green and a similarly dark blue if your complexion is medium.

If this sounds a little confusing, just start playing with it as if you were playing with paint on a canvas. As you experiment with contrast in your wardrobe choices, you'll notice what works and what doesn't, and you'll begin to get a feeling for what I mean.

Texture

Learning about my own degree of texture, and then learning how to mirror that degree of texture in my wardrobe choices, not only helped me feel great in my clothes, it also helped me feel great in my skin. I no longer felt like unruly hair and skin with occasional freckles, wrinkles, and ruddiness was something to be ashamed of, but rather traits that were not any more or less beautiful than smooth hair and uniform skin—just different. (Not that I don't still wear foundation or put smoothing potion in my hair—I do! I just feel a lot more comfortable with my starting point.)

So, what this means for you is: when you look at your complexion in the mirror, is it smooth and uniform in color? Or do you notice textures such as color variations, wrinkles, or freckles?

Also, when you look at your hair, is it glassy, shiny, straight, or smooth? Is it curly, wavy, unruly, or otherwise textured? Is it all the same color, or is it characterized by streaks, highlights, or lowlights?

When you get an idea for the degree of texture you possess in your skin and hair, you can choose wardrobe pieces that feel like natural continuations of this degree of texture.

The smoother, more uniform, and less textured you are, the better you will look and feel in:

- smooth, sleek fabrics such as satin and combed cotton

- minimal jewelry and accessories

- uniform or minimal textures or prints in one outfit

The more variety and dimension you have in your texture, the better you will look and feel in:

- highly textured fabrics such as crochet and lace

- a generous and varied selection of jewelry and accessories

- a variety of textures and/or prints all in one outfit

Another little note: embracing the texture of your hair and casting it in its best possible light via your wardrobe choices can help save your strands from the damaging effects of excessive heat styling.

Your Emotional Impact

Real art has a real emotional impact of some sort. And since you are a work of art, you are the same.

> In order to stay easily
> and happily creative,
> we need to stay
> spiritually centered.
> This is easier to do
> if we allow ourselves
> centering rituals.
>
> JULIA CAMERON, AUTHOR
> AND CREATIVITY EXPERT

While your moods can change with the weather—and your emotional impact may also shift over time—just like a painting, your very presence emits a particular flavor of poetry: a unique message and energetic signature.

So for this exercise, wear something neutral that you won't notice too much, or just go nude or wear your underwear. Light a candle and—if it feels right—listen to that playlist that you made. (Alternatively, simply play something relaxing and centering, such as classical or ambient music.) You might also want to light a stick of incense or diffuse a few drops of essential oil. Sit near the mirror again, and look into your eyes. Take some time to relax and get in touch with yourself.

Do your very best to gaze at yourself lovingly. Look at your physical traits, but also see beyond those and look into your heart and your essence. If you generally think or say negative things about yourself, and if these things are rising to the surface as you do this exercise, know that this only means that you aren't seeing your true essence, which is divinely designed—a lily of the field! So, right now, rise above those old habits to see yourself as the multi-layered artistic masterpiece that you are. This might mean that you need to give yourself some extra time to cry as you open your heart and acknowledge the pain of your less-than-complimentary body image or self-talk of the past. If this is the case, breathe consciously, sending breath to any spots in your body or spirit that feel painful or closed off. Then (even if it feels like a challenge or even if you have to do it through tears), when you feel open and loving, with the utmost respect for yourself, begin to ask the following questions, taking a bit of time to answer each in your journal.

- Knowing that I am a masterpiece, if I were a portrait—such as the Mona Lisa—what would I be feeling and thinking?
  — Where would I be sitting (or standing or reclining)?
  — What type of feeling would I give viewers?
- Knowing that I am a masterpiece, if I were a song, what type of feeling would I give the listener?
  — If I had lyrics, what would they be about?
  — What instruments would I feature?
- Knowing that I am a masterpiece, if I were a movie, what genre would I be?
  — What would the main character really, really want, or what lesson would she or he learn?

— Where would the movie be set?

— What themes or motifs would appear in the film?

- Knowing that I am a masterpiece, if I were a novel, what genre would I be?

  — In what time period would I be set?

  — What would my message or philosophy be?

  — What mood would I give the reader?

- Knowing that I am a masterpiece, if I were a poem, what words would compose me? (Or, if you don't want to write a poem, what are some of the main words that I would include?)

Please note that, although your unique essence has a fundamental continuity and core—just as your styles and habits change over time—your answers will vary if you approach this exercise at different times throughout your life. Nonetheless, at this particular moment on your personal timeline, you now have a clearer picture of the type of message that you (as the divine and masterful work of art that you are) visually and emotionally convey. So take a moment to integrate this picture. Let it roll around in your consciousness like a melody or a daydream for a little while. As you do this, you might want to dance or draw or try on outfits. Or perhaps you'll just want to lie around or gaze into your own eyes in the mirror or cry or hug yourself in silence. Do whatever feels right. Then, when you're ready, brainstorm about the following in your journal:

- What are five ways I might playfully integrate my emotional signature through my wardrobe?

- What are five wardrobe choices I might make to highlight and amplify my emotional impact?

- What are five wardrobe choices that might be fun?

- What aspects of my current wardrobe feel like they're in alignment with my essence?

- What aspects of my current wardrobe don't feel like they're in alignment with my essence?

- What are five ways to improve my life by honoring my unique beauty through my wardrobe choices every day?

"The Rules"

My mom fondly remembers an art professor who taught her that it's okay to break the rules, as long as you know them first, so that breaking a rule is a conscious choice rather than an unknowing faux pas. In a way, "fashion rules" are moot from the start, since styles are constantly in flux, not to mention that elegantly breaking a so-called rule is one of the most traditional ways to start a trend. Still, here is a sampling of some of the most enduring "rules." I'm including them because when you know them, in addition to following them in ways that feel right to you, you can also break them in good conscience.

Match your belt to your shoes and your shoes to your purse. Generally speaking, this is often a good idea: it just feels right and adds chic cohesion to an outfit. But there are also times when a conscious decision *not* to do so feels right too. Use your discretion.

There came
a point when I had
moved to Vegas, and I was sort
of unraveling, but I was also doing
stuff like journaling a lot, and I finally
started to understand the self-love thing.
I began to be much sweeter to myself. I
would take baths and say a mantra and think
positive thoughts about my toes (which I
had previously been really negative about).
And it was right around this time that I
saw "What the Bleep Do We Know,"
and I began to honor my body
as a temple a bit more.

JANINE JORDAN

Don't wear white after Labor Day or before Memorial Day. When we're talking about wearing white in that easy, breezy, summery way, this is generally a good rule of thumb because it feels right for the season. But when we're talking about wearing a fleecy white sweater or snowy, sparkly scarf to a holiday party, why on earth not? The trick is to make sure the material is season appropriate.

Don't mix prints. This one—considering the current fashion climate and from the perspective of a highly textured person (see above)—has got to go. But I will admit that mixing prints does require taste and artistic sensibility, so be mindful of your print-mixing choices. Mixing prints that are of a similar size and go together melodically is key, as is looking at the overall impact and unity of the ensemble. A good rule of thumb is to make sure that the color combos in each print are comparable in intensity.

Don't wear black and navy or black and brown together. I remember in the 1980s and '90s when this one used to seem to make sense, but now mixing these colors seems to look so right. Maybe it will go back out of style; I don't know.

Don't wear socks with open-toed shoes. As I mentioned above, sometimes a new trend is simply a conscious breaking of a fashion rule, as proven by the currently fashionable practice of wearing cute little bobby socks or tights with platform sandals. (Personally, I think it's sort of adorable.)

Be mindful of the current styles and trends. I used to be so embarrassed when my grandma would take me clothes shopping and ask the salesgirl things like "How are the girls wearing their shirts these days? Are they tucking them in?" At the time, I rebelled because I thought she was trying to make me into a good little cookie cutter. But now that I'm long out of high school, I understand her motivation a bit differently. As Chanel designer and fashion icon Karl Lagerfeld alluded to in the movie *Lagerfeld Confidential*, the quick turnaround of the fashion season can help one to stay fresh and present rather than stuck in any sort of artistic or personal rut. And while I am definitely not one to run out and buy a whole new wardrobe every season, I do find that being aware of what's going on in the current fashion season can be a great way to stay awake to my own personal shifts and the shifts in the collective consciousness; it also affirms and bolsters my desire to keep growing and learning and changing. Of course, if I don't like something, I won't do it, but if picking up a fashion magazine or perusing a street fashion blog can help me think of new and fun ways to wear a belt or accessorize (for example), then I am all for it.

It's important to remember that, when it comes to adorning our own bodies, "We are the music makers, and we are the dreamers of the dreams" (in the words of Willy Wonka)—not the fashion designers or the magazine editors. So if we don't like what "everyone" is supposed to be wearing or we want to wear something in a way that is currently against the so-called rules, we must honor our own personality and unique sense of style. Giorgio Armani summarized it well when he said, "Say to yourself, 'I know what I like, and if fashion proposes something that's not me, forget it.'"

I think it's a wonderful
opportunity to share
the essence of who I am
through what I wear, but
I do my best to avoid the
cultural trap of letting my
appearance become my
identity. I want to be able
to walk into a room in my
PJs if needed and still be
authentic and confident.

RACHEL AVALON, HOLISITIC HEALTH
COACH AND ECO-EXPERT

A Bit of Practicality

Here is an essential bit of tried-and-true, practical fashion wisdom: keep in mind that having a solid selection of multi-use, neutral pieces is an excellent strategy for most wardrobes. So, for example, you might determine that for your lifestyle, look, and unique personal essence, your foundational pieces might include:

Jeans

Neutral and/or black slacks

Khakis

A few black tank tops or camisoles

A few white T-shirts

A long black skirt

A short black skirt

A flowing neutral skirt

A little black dress

An off-white button-down shirt

A black belt

A brown belt

A trench coat

A pea coat

Nude heels

Brown sandals

Sneakers

Ballet flats

Black boots

Necessary bras, slips, tights,
and other undergarments

When it comes to your foundational pieces, it's a good idea to take your time and find items of quality. You might even spend a few extra bucks if the situation calls for it, since you could conceivably have each piece for years and wear it frequently. (Although if you happen to find some of them at a thrift store, discount store, or clothing swap, that's excellent too!) Making sure these pieces are just right is what will make your wardrobe look like a million bucks.

Again, these might vary: only you will know what fits you. For example, a number of fashion books and articles insist that every woman needs at least one pair of stilettos. Considering my casual California lifestyle and the fact that I haven't yet bonded with stilettos in any way, this was initially very confusing to me. In fact, as of this writing I have never in my entire life felt particularly drawn to them. Wedge sandals, however, I adore.

As you get to know your personal essence and assess your lifestyle through working with the ideas and journaling exercises in this book, you'll start to have a clear picture of the neutral basics that you already have in your closet, as well as the ones you still need. The idea is to have essential pieces that will provide the backbone and attractively fill in the gaps of any given outfit. So perhaps reserve a page in your notebook or journal for a running tally of what these may be.

Once you finalize your list and then acquire a good selection of foundational pieces that you absolutely love, you can then rotate things like sweaters, scarves, vests, accessories, and other stand-out pieces to facilitate high degrees of wardrobe efficiency and versatility. Every few years or so, you might feel motivated to upgrade the foundational pieces as your tastes and preferences change.

Waste Not, Want Not
A WORD ON CONSCIOUS ACQUIRING

Two of my best girlfriends are both super stylish and super eco-friendly.

Rachel Avalon, *eco-expert, might be called the clothing swap queen of Los Angeles. Here's what she has to say about them:*

"Easily 90 percent of my clothes, shoes, and accessories are from clothing swaps. I started hosting the parties because I was so disturbed by sweatshops and the environmental impact of buying new clothes, and I didn't have the interest in going to a lot of organic, alternative boutiques. I had grown up buying clothes at thrift stores and such, but it was so time consuming to find the sizes and styles I was looking for. I had grown accustomed to buying a lot of new things that I couldn't really justify given my awareness and values…Once I made the decision to host and attend clothing swaps instead, my whole world changed. I was able to not only find almost everything I needed from my girlfriends and their friends, I was able to experience their gratitude of finding 'new' clothes and building a stronger community. What's incredible is that as much as we pick out,

we always have about ten bags to donate when we're done. So these clothing swaps accomplish quite a bit. We reduce labor exploitation, environmental destruction, consumerism, and spending, and we help others in need...all while having a great time with each other. If everyone attended at least two clothing swap a year, it'd be revolutionary."

Janine Jordan, *eco-activist and founder of a nonprofit called Greenwave, says:*

"I really appreciate going to thrift shops and having friends who are the same size and swapping clothes with them. I am very aware of the environmental impact of the fashion industry, so I really prefer to find things that are already created. Or, if I'm thinking of getting something new, I'll look for a smaller designer and something that I know is created with more respect for the environment. It's important for me to be more sensitive about my choices, because I know that small choices make a big impact cumulatively."

A Word on Acquiring

Assembling a wardrobe is like planning and enjoying a meal: you want to have enough, but not too much. So, for example, when I consider having more than one pair of dressy boots or an extra short black skirt, it just doesn't feel right. Too much stuff equals too little serenity and too much closet confusion. As Francine Jay emphasizes on her blog and in her lovely e-book of the same name, *Miss Minimalist*, having

When I
would go shopping
years ago, I would feel so
down if I tried something on that
I thought was really cute but just
wasn't flattering on me. If I was only
more this or that, maybe it would look
better. Now I am much more accepting
of the fact that not every style looks
good on every body. Now that I have
a better handle on what works
on me, I rock those items.

ERIN JANE AMABILE,
MAGICAL FASHIONISTA

less can feel so much more pleasing—and liberating—than having more. So with this in mind, get rid of what you don't love so that you have room for what you *do* love, and then keep it to what I like to call "an elegant minimum."

What's more, when you're shopping or considering what you want at a clothing swap, wait until it clicks. You know that feeling you get when you think that perhaps you should buy a particular item, but you're also sweating and worrying and generally feeling uncomfortable about it? That's your intuition telling you not to get it. No matter what your intellect tells you, your gut knows better. Just hang it back up where you found it and walk away. You'll see: in a very short time, if a similar item would indeed be perfect for your wardrobe, you'll find or acquire one that's much better or much less expensive or both. And rather than feeling stress, you'll feel joy and expansion at the prospect of bringing it home.

3

you are

AN INTERPLAY OF ELEMENTS

From tarot to astrology, acupuncture to feng shui, the elements of nature play a leading role in mystical cosmologies and healing modalities, both Eastern and Western. And magical fashion is no different.

When it comes to the unique interplay of elements that is you, what elements predominate, and how do they interact with each other? What's more, how can you utilize fashion choices that draw upon these elements to enhance your beauty and help magnetize the conditions you desire? These questions, and the answers to them, are the topic of this chapter.

You'll notice that I've included two separate elemental systems: Western (which is generally composed of four elements) and Eastern (which is composed of five). I find that

One of the ideas that has run deeply and persistently through Western occultism is that of the four Elements: Air, Fire, Water, and Earth. The ancients believed literally that all substance was made of these.

TERESA MOOREY, AUTHOR OF *THE FAIRY BIBLE*

According to Chinese energy theory, everything in the universe is made up of varying combinations of five elements, or forms of energy.

DAVID DANIEL KENNEDY, AUTHOR AND FENG SHUI EXPERT

You Are an Interplay of Elements

the Western elemental system is an excellent tool for getting acquainted with our primary motivations and preferences, while the Eastern, or Chinese, elemental system provides a practical framework for dynamic, intentional interaction with things in the physical world (such as your wardrobe and life conditions).

Western Astrology and You

"What's your sign?" What we generally mean when we ask this question is "What's your sun sign?" or "What astrological sign was the sun in on the day that you were born?" Even those of us who aren't terribly familiar with astrology generally know our sun sign. You also may know that each sign possesses a particular elemental association, but in case you're not sure:

Taurus, Virgo, and Capricorn are earth signs.

Gemini, Libra, and Aquarius are air signs.

Cancer, Scorpio, and Pisces are water signs.

Leo, Sagittarius, and Aries are fire signs.

Although the element related to your sun sign is just the tip of the iceberg, it does reveal a lot. The sun is the most powerful influence from a Western astrological perspective, so it's a pretty broad brushstroke. Elementally speaking, it has to do with how your nature seeks to express itself in the world. (You'll get an idea of what I mean as we continue.) The wardrobe selections are just to awaken you to possibilities: you may resonate with some and not with others.

Please keep in mind that there are countless other factors that make you unique (including your Chinese sign and elemental makeup, which you'll be learning a lot more about later). So when you read the descriptions in this section, perhaps make a note of the things that ring a bell and ignore the others or just keep them in the back of your mind as you proceed through the remainder of the book. You might, for example, determine that even though you're an earth sign, your most prominent element is fire. Or you might discover that incorporating more water into your wardrobe will help balance you in the way you've been craving. So, as you read, keep an open mind and consider all the factors at work.

Earth signs enjoy connecting with nature and the physical world: you feel at home gardening, walking in nature, and enjoying sensual pleasures such as food, texture, and scent.

If you're an earth sign, you may enjoy:

- earth tones: shades of earthy purple, brown, terra cotta, and tan

- cozy, comfy, nature-inspired styles

- earthy gems such as agate, jasper, and carnelian

- natural fabrics like cotton and bamboo

Air signs are about thoughts, words, and the imagination. Your mind moves quickly, like the breeze, and you have a particular fondness for winged creatures and flying vehicles.

If you're an air sign, you may enjoy:

- airy colors: white, off-white, silver, sky blue, and light gray

- simple, breezy styles

- airy gems such as quartz, fluorite, and larimar

- flip-flops, sandals, and things that sparkle or shine

Water signs are emotional and intuitive. Dreams, underwater scenes and creatures, and fluid movements all belong in your realm.

If you're a water sign, you may enjoy:

- watery colors: blue, black, green, and white

- dramatic or mermaid-inspired styles

- watery gems like aquamarine, sodalite, and moonstone

- draped or cascading fabric

Fire signs express passion and shine light brightly in the world. Like flames, you enjoy dancing, moving, and glowing radiantly for all to see.

If you're a fire sign, you may enjoy:

- fiery colors: reds, pinks, and oranges

- fun, sassy, sparkly, and daring styles

- fiery gems like opal, ruby, and tiger's-eye

- daring, unique ensembles and things you can dance in

> I love sparkles, and
> I definitely went through
> a phase when I wanted red
> everything and wore dark
> pink lipstick all the time.
>
> JANINE JORDAN, ARIES

To learn more about your Western astrological elemental makeup, I suggest also taking into account your moon sign and your rising sign, both of which indicate strong undercurrents in your personality. If you don't already know what these are, there are a number of sites where you can type in your birth information and discover these signs for free online, and you might also like to check out *The Only Astrology Book You'll Ever Need* by Joanne Martine Woolfolk.

Chinese Astrology and You

Fashions and attitudes continually seem to move through the planet like flowing tides. This year pencil skirts might be all the rage, and then next year it's micro-minis. Suddenly, it seems like everyone wants to watch movies and documentaries about Paris in the 1920s or dinosaurs or zombies or the

Titanic. There is a flavor of the times, a unique zeitgeist that seems to tune everyone to a particular frequency—a fluid emanation that almost seems to radiate outward from the core of the earth. As a matter of fact, in addition to being the invisible catalyst for the kaleidoscopic fashions, ideas, and obsessions that characterize the day, the cycling emanation of earth energies is the basis of Chinese astrology. Additionally, the Chinese five-element system teaches us how we can alchemically interact with these energies in order to create greater levels of harmony, balance, beauty, and success.

The Chinese elemental system, which is a core component of feng shui, acupuncture, and Chinese astrology, is composed of five elements: fire, earth, metal, water, and wood.

If you don't already know your Chinese sign, I highly recommend finding it out and learning about it. (My favorite books on the topic are *The Handbook of Chinese Horoscopes* by Theodora Lau and *The New Chinese Astrology* by Suzanne White.) But for the purposes of this book, all we'll be looking at is your element (rather than your sign). So, if you don't already know your element (or even perhaps if you think you do, just so you can be sure), find yourself below:

You've got a lot of the fire element in your makeup if you were born between:

February 3, 1916 and February 10, 1918
February 13, 1926 and January 22, 1928
January 24, 1936 and January 30, 1938
February 2, 1946 and February 9, 1948
February 12, 1956 and February 17, 1958

January 21, 1966 and January 29, 1968

January 31, 1976 and February 6, 1978

February 9, 1986 and February 16, 1988

February 19, 1996 and January 27, 1998

January 29, 2006 and February 6, 2008

You've got a lot of the earth element in your makeup if you were born between:

February 11, 1918 and February 19, 1920

January 23, 1928 and January 29, 1930

January 31, 1938 and February 7, 1940

February 10, 1948 and February 16, 1950

February 18, 1958 and January 27, 1960

January 30, 1968 and February 5, 1970

February 7, 1978 and February 15, 1980

February 17, 1988 and January 26, 1990

January 28, 1998 and February 4, 2000

February 7, 2008 and February 13, 2010

You've got a lot of the metal element in your makeup if you were born between:

February 20, 1920 and January 27, 1922

January 30, 1930 and February 5, 1932

February 8, 1940 and February 14, 1942

February 17, 1950 and January 26, 1952

January 28, 1960 and February 4, 1962

February 6, 1970 and February 15, 1972

February 16, 1980 and January 24, 1982

January 27, 1990 and February 3, 1992

> *February 5, 2000 and February 11, 2002*
> *February 14, 2010 and January 22, 2012*

You've got a lot of the water element in your makeup if you were born between:

> *February 18, 1912 and January 25, 1914*
> *January 28, 1922 and February 4, 1924*
> *February 6, 1932 and February 13, 1934*
> *February 15, 1942 and January 24, 1944*
> *January 27, 1952 and February 2, 1954*
> *February 5, 1962 and February 12, 1964*
> *February 15, 1972 and January 22, 1974*
> *January 25, 1982 and February 1, 1984*
> *February 4, 1992 and February 9, 1994*
> *February 12, 2002 and January 21, 2004*
> *January 23, 2012 and January 30, 2014*

You've got a lot of the wood element in your makeup if you were born between:

> *January 26, 1914 and February 2, 1916*
> *February 5, 1924 and February 12, 1926*
> *February 14, 1934 and January 23, 1936*
> *January 25, 1944 and February 1, 1946*
> *February 3, 1954 and February 11, 1956*
> *February 13, 1964 and January 20, 1966*
> *January 23, 1974 and January 30, 1976*
> *February 2, 1984 and February 8, 1986*
> *February 10, 1994 and February 18, 1996*
> *January 22, 2004 and January 28, 2006*

You Are an Interplay of Elements

As I mentioned above, none of us is any one element alone: we are each an utterly unique interplay of a number of elements. Still, your Chinese element is most likely one of the strongest factors in your elemental makeup. The descriptions below are quintessential aspects of each element. If you don't recognize yourself at all in yours, withhold judgment for a while as you continue to work with the ideas in this book and chip away at the divine mystery that is you. As you do, you may just find yourself aligning more and more with your native element. (Or you might discover another element that is totally "you.")

Fire Fashions

Fire people like to dance, express, sparkle, shine, and be center stage. You have a lot of passion, and you feel in your element when you're in the midst of any sort of outward expression or social interaction.

Wardrobe additions that enhance your elemental essence include:

- things that sparkle and shine

- animal prints and faux animal materials (faux leather, fur, silk)

- fun jewelry (animal-shaped pendants, feather-shaped pendants, oversized rings, etc.)

- boas, scarves, or whatever makes you feel like a movie star

- star shapes, triangle shapes, radial shapes, and zigzags

- pointy, flashy, or high-heeled shoes

- reds, pinks, purples, and bright oranges

- anything that might be described as "fun" or "hot"

Earth Fashions

Earth people enjoy tradition, cozy nights in, cooking, and spending time in the garden and nature. You are nurturing, generous, and family-oriented, and you feel in your element when you're helping others.

Wardrobe additions that enhance your elemental essence include:

- earth tones such as beige, brown, tan, earthy purple, yellow, cream, burnt orange, and terra cotta

- comfy and natural fiber fabrics like corduroy, flannel, and cotton

- square shapes such as plaid or checkered prints

- traditional styles and styles that remind you of the way people dress in your hometown

- classic pieces like khakis, simply patterned dresses, and button-down shirts

- clogs, flats, and square-toed, comfy shoes

- anything that might be described as "cozy" or "classic"

Metal Fashions

Metal people love precision, simplicity, elegance, scientific or other thought-oriented pursuits, and travel. You're sharp as a tack, you've got an uncommon eye for detail, and you're in your element when your mind is at work.

Wardrobe additions that enhance your elemental essence include:

- light, solid neutrals such as white, cream, light gray, and light beige

- dark, solid neutrals such as black, navy blue, and charcoal gray

- metallic colors and accents, especially silver, platinum, and gold

- designer clothes or clothes that are extremely well tailored and pristine

- classic, simple pieces such as a little black dress or a gray business suit

- round or oval shapes such as tasteful polka dots

- simple, timeless pieces

- minimal accessories and sleek styles

- anything that might be described as "sharp" or "clean"

Water Fashions

Water people flow with life: your heart flows with emotion, your mind flows with possibilities, and your spirit flows into the depths of both joy and heartbreak, although all of this happens very deeply and in an isolated way, so you don't always share all of this with others. You are in your element when you're dreaming, meditating, resting, or creating art of any kind.

Wardrobe additions that enhance your elemental essence include:

- deep, dark colors like black, chocolate, and navy blue

- flowy items such as skirts and scarves

- romantic, unique, foreign, artsy styles

- asymmetrical shapes, wavy lines, and teardrop shapes

- reflective accents such as mirrored pendants, glass buttons, or fabric with silvery shimmers

- silver jewelry

- dark sunglasses

- anything that might be described as "free" or "cool"

Wood Fashions

Wood people love self-improvement activities such as exercise, study, and all forms of personal growth. Like a healthy plant, you are always reaching upwards, toward the light. You're in your element when you're working out, learning something new, achieving great things, or climbing a mountain (literally or figuratively).

Wardrobe additions that enhance your elemental essence include:

- sneakers, sporty sandals, and other shoes you can move in

- action-friendly wear like sweats, safari clothes, or yoga gear

- shades of blue and green

- vertical stripes and floral prints

- leaf, tree, or flower shapes

- wood accents such as jewelry or buttons

- plant-derived fabrics such as cotton and bamboo

- straw hats

- functional features such as drawstrings and pockets

- anything that might be described as "sporty" or "natural"

Beyond Your Birthday: The Five Elements and You

The five-element system shows up in every single thing. Literally. Not just horoscopes, colors, textures, and shapes, but also sounds, thoughts, situations, music, flavors, personality traits, qualities of movement, building materials, the natural world, and everything else you can imagine. In fact, all five elements are present within your being in some combination. Here, you'll get a lot more acquainted with how the five elements appear in your unique elemental makeup, and you'll learn how you can consciously affect your personal balance of elements in order to feel beautiful, be beautiful, and magnetize the conditions you desire.

Fire Characteristics

Facial characteristics that indicate the fire element include:

- anything that appears pointy or triangular: nose, chin, eyebrow shape, upper crests of lips, or face shape in general

- dimples

- a cleft chin

- warmth in the eye color: golden brown or violet blue

- eyes that appear to glow from within

- pinkish or reddish tones in the skin and a tendency to flush

Hair characteristics that indicate the fire element include:

- red hair or a reddish undertone

- curly hair

- unruly hair

- wavy hair with a lot of texture (but not smooth, cascading waves—that's the water element)

Body characteristics that indicate the fire element include:

- broad shoulders and strong back with a more tapered waist and hips

- a strong, powerful feeling to one's movement

Personality traits that indicate the fire element include:

- an extremely animated way of speaking

- a high, melodious voice

- a burning desire for attention

- a natural ability to perform or lead

- flirtatiousness

- joy in social interaction

- an overriding need for fun

If you recognize that you have a lot of the fire element in your natural makeup, it will feel good to you to incorporate some of the wardrobe hints in the previous "Fire Fashions" section, provided you feel drawn to them. You might also want to employ some aspects of fire in your wardrobe if your intentions for the day or for your current life situation include any of the following:

- feeling more comfortable with public speaking or performing of any kind

- stepping out of the shadows and letting your light shine: i.e., following your bliss in a visible way that will attract attention and admiration

- a more active or enjoyable social life

- having fun

- feeling energized and playful

Earth Characteristics

Facial characteristics that indicate the earth element include:

- a rounded yet somewhat square-shaped face

- square-shaped features such as chin or jaw

- a full upper eyelid area

- a larger mouth (in comparison to the rest of your face)

- a prominent bridge of the nose

- full lips

- full lower cheeks

- brown, hazel, or golden tones in eyes

- golden, brown, or yellow tone to skin

Hair characteristics that indicate the earth element include:

- brown, yellow, or golden tones

- thick, abundant hair

Body characteristics that indicate the earth element include:

- a rounded belly

- upper and lower body somewhat proportional to each other

Personality traits that indicate the earth element include:

- a very deep desire to nurture

- loyalty to one's family and home

- a love of food: preparing, eating, and sharing with others

- a tendency to put others' needs above your own

- an ability to get very calm and quiet

- a love of gardening and resting outdoors

- a love of tradition

If you recognize that you have a lot of the earth element in your natural makeup, it will feel good to you to incorporate some of the wardrobe hints from the previous "Earth Fashions" section, provided you feel drawn to them. You might also want to employ some aspects of earth in your wardrobe if your intentions for the day or for your current life situation include any of the following:

- conception of a child

- nurturing others

- healing family issues

- feeling safe

- enhancing a feeling of coziness in your home and life

- feeling still, grounded, and serene

Metal Characteristics

Facial characteristics that indicate the metal element include:

- prominent cheekbones

- narrow yet prominent nose

- raised moles

- light-toned skin (for your ethnic background)

- sparkly white teeth

- pale eyes or eyes with gray undertones

Hair characteristics that indicate the metal element include:

- light or ashy tones

- gray or silver hair

- wiry or stick-straight hair

Body characteristics that indicate the metal element include:

- graceful, controlled movements

- naturally thin frame

Personality traits that indicate the metal element include:

- attention to detail and efficiency

- an elegant bearing and demeanor

- cleanliness and minimalism

- always taking whatever time or money necessary to "do it right" (whatever "it" may be)

- a sharp mind and quick wit

- an uncommon capacity for sustained focus

- a notable intelligence

If you recognize that you have a lot of the metal element in your natural makeup, it will feel good to you to incorporate some of the wardrobe hints from the previous "Metal Fashions" section, provided you feel drawn to them. You might also want to employ some aspects of metal in your wardrobe if your intentions for the day or for your current life situation include any of the following:

- moving up the corporate or social ladder

- scientific pursuits

- working with computers, vehicles, or mechanical items

- anything that requires precision and a sharp, focused mind

- simplifying and streamlining

- travel and communication

Water Characteristics

Facial characteristics that indicate the water element include:

- rounded or teardrop-shaped features: nose, chin, eyes, cheeks, or general face shape

- big eyes

- shadowed eyes

- prominent earlobes

- very dark brown or blue eyes

- rounded, prominent forehead

Hair characteristics that indicate the water element include:

- dark hair color

- flowing, cascading hair

- shiny hair

- smooth, wavy hair

Body characteristics that indicate the water element include:

- thighs and hips wider in comparison to upper body

- smooth, flowing, or gliding quality to movements

Personality traits that indicate the water element include:

- unconventional, romantic, artistic approach to life

- dreaminess

- deep, heartfelt emotional experience that you sometimes have trouble expressing in words (or don't express in words)

- preference for being alone

You Are an Interplay of Elements

- preference for softer lighting and darker environments

- notable artistic proclivities

If you recognize that you have a lot of the water element in your natural makeup, it will feel good to you to incorporate some of the wardrobe hints from the previous "Water Fashions" section, provided you feel drawn to them. You might also want to employ some aspects of water in your wardrobe if your intentions for the day or for your current life situation include any of the following:

- artistic, creative, imaginative pursuits

- following the flow of your authentic life path

- flowing with your passion

- feeling your feelings

- getting more sleep

- feeling free

- expressing your uniqueness

- stepping out of "same old, same old"

Wood Characteristics

Facial characteristics that indicate the wood element include:

- prominent eyebrows or brow bone

- a prominent jaw

- chiseled features

- blue or green eyes, or eyes with green tones

- an olive-undertoned complexion

Hair characteristics that indicate the wood element include:

- thick, fast-growing hair

- tones or textures that are evocative of natural wood

Body characteristics that indicate the wood element include:

- natural athleticism and coordination

- a naturally willowy or muscular frame

- a tendency to want to keep moving

Personality traits that indicate the wood element include:

- a general desire to do things quickly and get things done

- a natural, seemingly constant drive to improve oneself through learning, exercising, eating well, and other self-growth endeavors

- enthusiasm, idealism, and curiosity

- a strong degree of natural health and immunity

If you recognize that you have a lot of the wood element in your natural makeup, it will feel good to you to incorporate some of the wardrobe hints from the previous "Wood Fashions" section, provided you feel drawn to them. You might also want to employ some aspects of wood in your

You Are an Interplay of Elements

wardrobe if your intentions for the day or for your current life situation include any of the following:

- weight loss or strength training

- sports or exercise

- meditation

- study

- activism

- having more natural energy and enthusiasm

- health

Practical Elemental Observations

Now that you've gotten a taste of the elements and how they appear within people and wardrobes, let's ground this information in your consciousness by taking a look at some familiar situations and styles. For example:

- Rock stars and pop sensations often exhibit a style that screams fire (shiny fabrics, leather, brightness) but possesses strong secondary aspects of water (black, asymmetry, drama). This makes sense since these lifestyles are about both fame and artistic endeavors.

- Country stars, on the other hand, are usually found wearing a combination of earth (more "down home" styles such as jeans, boots, and simple dress patterns) and fire (sequins, eye-catching colors, pointy boots or shoes), which also makes sense since country stars are, of course, famous (which relates to fire), while their songs have more traditional roots and focus more on topics such as relationships, family, and home (all related to earth).

- Preppy style—named after prep school—is essentially a combination of wood and metal, with strong undercurrents of earth: a natural match for the values of your average prep school attendee: learning and sports (wood), precision and clear thinking (metal), and making one's family proud (earth).

- Lab coats are white (the metal element) and are employed in situations that require cleanliness, scientific prowess, and a pristine attention to detail, all of which are associated with the metal element.

- Goth style emphasizes black, drama, and uniqueness, and often includes asymmetrical aspects: an extreme example of the angst and poeticism of the water element.

A Few More Words on the Elements

Most likely, you will have just discovered some of each element present in yourself to some degree. Obviously, this is not a "paint by numbers" sort of thing: it's more about being conscious of how the elements appear within you and in the physical world. This way, you're empowered to incorporate wardrobe choices that both enhance your natural energy and lend fuel to your goals and desires.

If it feels overwhelming, don't worry: perhaps just jot down a few notes and take it slow. See if you can begin to notice the five elements at work in your friends and family, magazine and fashion blog photos (TheSartorialist.com is my—and almost everyone else's—favorite), and even the people you see on the street. Also take a look at the items in your present wardrobe and see which elemental categories they may fall into. For example, you may have a flowing skirt that's made of a cotton fabric with an animal print. The fact that it's a flowing skirt makes it watery. The cotton fabric is the wood element, and the animal print is fire: so this isn't just one element, it's three. If the animal print is mostly gold and brown, it's also earth. And if there are hints of cream in the print—or perhaps a couple of silver buttons—it's got some metal as well. So, as you can see, it's conceivable that you'll have some pieces that incorporate a bit of each element.

Still, you will begin to perceive that each garment and outfit—and perhaps even your entire wardrobe—has a particular elemental flavor. Maybe your wardrobe is generally earthy, with an undercurrent of wood. Or maybe your wardrobe features a lot of watery elements with an overarching flavor of fire. The elemental system is a language, and now that you know about it, your awareness and understanding of it will deepen and gain dimension throughout your lifetime.

4

you are
EXACTLY WHERE YOU'RE SUPPOSED TO BE

When I was in high school, the grunge look was all the rage. And let me tell you, the weirder-the-better fashions of the time were a dream for a small-town, offbeat girl with not very much money: I could get all my shopping done at thrift stores and feel effortlessly edgy and hip. What, the popular kids snickered when I walked into the room? Good, I thought. It meant that I was doing something right.

After that—especially when I moved out of the small country town and into a huge city by my wide-eyed, eighteen-year-old, almost-totally-broke self—things went downhill for me in the fashion department for a regrettably large number of years. Among other factors (including the ones

> If you want to look
> beautiful, you have
> to be confident.
> Diane von Furstenberg

cited in the first chapter of this book), I attribute this to the realization that in a big city there is the option of spending upwards of hundreds of dollars for any given clothing item or accessory, and the feeling that there was so much depth, complexity, and "insider"-ness to the fashion industry that I couldn't possibly hope to measure up. Frankly, I was intimidated. Finally, though, I've come to realize that fashion is accessible to everyone and that it's everyone's right to look good regardless of budget, adherence to trends, or the means to employ a stylist. Today, I am happy to report that I generally feel comfortable in my skin and in my clothes.

So, in conclusion, shocking my grandma and making the popular kids snicker isn't the point of fashion for me anymore, and neither is it the point to impress anyone with my designer duds or perfectly posh ensembles. Now, it's about feeling like myself—my most joyful, flowy, beautiful, mag-

You Are Exactly Where You're Supposed to Be

ical self—and wearing clothes and accessories that are in harmony with me, where I am, what I'm doing, and what I'd like to experience. When I feel that my clothes are enhancing my life experience in this way, I naturally radiate confidence and beauty, and I naturally enjoy my day a whole lot more than I otherwise would. Plus, this makes fashion a servant to me, rather than the other way around.

Confidence Picker-Uppers

Wear fabulous lingerie that you totally love. (For example, when underwear shopping, you might tune in to your inner little girl or inner adolescent who is beyond excited to get to wear sexy, cool, beautiful "grown up" panties.)

If you don't feel like you belong or you don't feel qualified, for just a moment, behave as if you do—then continue. Ask yourself, "How would I feel (and dress) if I knew this was exactly where I was supposed to be?"

Exude confidence in the way you move. Keep your spine straight, elongate your torso, open your heart, swing your hips, and luxuriate in the feeling of being in your body. Your mind will quickly follow suit. (More on this later.)

Do something that scares you a little but that is within the bounds of safety: take a belly dancing class, go to a party where you don't know everyone, or apply for a dream job. Regardless of the outcome, jumping the hurdle will immediately help you feel more confident.

73

Find a hat or scarf or pair of sunglasses that instantly makes you feel more mysterious, glamorous, and confident, then wear as needed.

As quickly as you can, and without stopping if possible, write an entire notebook page full of your most wonderful aspects: things you are proud of, things you are grateful for about yourself, compliments you've received, goals you've accomplished, risks you've taken, things that make you unique.

Clear all clutter out of your wardrobe (see chapter 1).

Feel Good Doing What You're Doing

Right before my first book came out, I remember dreading my book release party and a major book conference that my publisher had invited me to. When I really thought about it, though, I realized that quite possibly the main thing I was dreading was getting dressed up and having to appear in clothes I felt awkward in. That was a turning point for me: in that moment I saw very clearly the importance of feeling right in my clothes. Once I found some accessories and dresses that felt fun and empowering for my author events, I looked forward to the events with gusto and enjoyed them heartily. Even today, when I am invited to do an event, I get an exhilarating charge of joyful anticipation when I take the time to assemble an outfit that feels perfect for the occasion.

The moral of this story is this: if you're feeling uncomfortable or self-conscious, sure, you can imagine everyone else in their underwear, as Marsha does in *The Brady Bunch*.

But that's sort of creepy and not particularly delightful. Instead, why not take the time to the find clothes that highlight your radiance, and fuel your feeling that you are in the perfect place at the perfect time, doing exactly what you most want to be doing? Then everyone wins.

Also consider what you do on a regular basis so that you can be sure to have the clothing choices that will support your everyday fabulousness, no matter what the occasion. And may I suggest feeling great even in pajamas, workout wear, grocery store apparel, and housecleaning attire? You're going to be doing that stuff either way, so why not? Seriously, don't postpone your joy: wear stuff that makes you feel good.

Just to clarify about the whole housecleaning attire thing: I'm not suggesting that you make your casual/at-home wardrobe one more thing to stress out over! Just, you know, do it out of joy. If it feels natural and easy, maybe you could forgo the torn-up sweats for a sweet little cotton sundress or something. But if you'd rather not bother with the sundress some days, that's fine too. All I'm asking is that you make conscious, self-adoring decisions rather than assuming that it's your lot in life to wear stuff that doesn't enhance your experience of life. It might even simply mean the difference between a slightly ill-fitting T-shirt and a hip-in-a-disheveled-way T-shirt in a color you're in the mood for. Or you might want to consider...

Being a Goddess Every Day

My friend Sedona Soulfire's life (and style!) was changed forever when she went to India for three months. She explains:

I've always (really, always!) been attracted to flowy clothes that might be described as goddessy or priestessy. Then, in India, I saw women fully blinged out no matter what they were doing, dressed in the most beautiful saris, with all of their makeup and jewelry on— even if they were picking rice in the middle of a field or cleaning the back of a shop or selling oranges in a fruit stand on the street! Here in the US, I feel like there's a little bit of a stigma attached to things like wearing beautiful dresses to go hiking or lipstick to at the laundromat, like "why is she trying so hard?" And I believe that is a sad byproduct of the emphasis being too much on the masculine side of things.

So now, when I get dressed and when I'm choosing my clothes, I think, "How do I want to decorate the temple?" Of course, I want it to look and feel beautiful! So, for me, that manifests in flowy garments, scarves, jewelry, makeup, and sparkles. Since I've been back from India, I don't go out without beautiful scarves, and I don't go out without my jewelry...

Or Maybe You Want to Be Invisible

On the other hand, if you're like many of us, there might be times when you want to go out and do stuff, but you don't particularly want to be noticed. My dear and often glamorous friend Janine Jordan has a beanie for those moments. She says:

> When I don't want anyone to talk to me, I might put a beanie on and I might not brush my hair, because I don't want people to pay attention to me. I've learned how to dress down so that people don't bother me. It's sort of like how people sometimes wear headphones these days, almost as if to say, "Don't talk to me, I'm not interested, I'm busy, I'm on a mission."

I usually consider three elements when choosing what to wear: intuition, how I'll be spending my day, and the weather. I let my intuition guide me to colors, styles, and textures that strengthen and balance me and reflect specific energies I want to share with others. I tend to have a lot of teal in my wardrobe since it combines colors from the heart and throat chakras. I also have a good amount of purples and lavenders to inspire myself and the people around me to think and act from their true, conscious self.

RACHEL AVALON,
HOLISTIC HEALTH COACH AND ECO-EXPERT

Wear a Number of Hats

Most of us treasure at least one major role in our life, whether that role is mother, partner, entrepreneur, belly dancer, or schoolteacher. But we are so much more than that one role! When we get the idea that we are just one thing (e.g., "Who am I? I'm a grandma" or "Who am I? I'm a college student"), we can begin to feel stifled and stagnant because we are not expressing the full, sparkling, multifaceted nature of the jewel that we are.

For example, in addition to your role as "grandma" or "college student," you might also have facets that resemble any number of the following:

- a sex kitten

- a flower child

- a salsa dancer

- a poet

- a folk musician

- a comic book enthusiast

- an anarchist

- a wine aficionado

- a hopeless romantic

So grab your journal and a pen and let's jump right into the following journal exercise.

Number 1–5. Without thinking too much about it, list five facets of your personality. Draw inspiration from the facets listed before or think of your own. If you don't think you have five, just "pretend" for a moment that you do.

Number 6–10. Now list five facets of your personality that you wish you had or that you would like to cultivate more of. If you can't think of any, for now, again, let's just pretend. (If you did wish you had a particular facet, what would it be? Classical guitarist? Vegan sushi chef? Kickboxer?)

Number 11–15. Think of at least one person that you are either bitterly jealous of or whom you deeply admire. (More than one is fine too.) Now list five facets that you perceive this person (or these people) to possess. If you don't know of five facets, imagine what they might be if you did know them.

Number 16–20. Think of at least one famous person that you would like to meet. List five facets that you perceive this person (or people) to possess. Again, if you don't know of five facets that this person possesses, just make them up: what would they be if you *did* know them?

Now, without numbering, see if you can dredge up any other facets of you and write them down, brainstorm-style.

Take a look at all the things you've written down. No matter which section you were responding to, and no matter whether you thought you were pretending or making something up or not, these are all roles that are present within you to some extent. Some of them you will currently be embracing or embodying, and some of them might seem foreign to you at this stage. Take a moment to consider each

You Are Exactly Where You're Supposed to Be

and notice how it's showing up in your personality and self-expression at this period in your life.

Now, with each and every facet you wrote down, think of a wardrobe choice that you might incorporate to begin to embody this facet more. The point of this is not to force yourself to do things you wouldn't normally want to do but to play with some ideas that might add dimension, flair, and enjoyment to your fashion choices and your day. So, for example, for the facets I listed above, you might write:

- a sex kitten: shorter skirts, fun lingerie, bright lipstick

- a flower child: long dresses, funky jewelry

- a salsa dancer: fitted dresses I can move in, platform heels, a push-up bra

- a poet: glasses, a flowy scarf, a quirky hat

- a folk musician: a long sweater with a hood and bell sleeves, a beanie

- a comic book enthusiast: a lace-up vest, tall heeled boots, a purple streak in my hair

- an anarchist: a nose ring, combat boots, a T-shirt with a radical message

- a wine aficionado: an elegant wide-brimmed hat, a burgundy scarf

- a hopeless romantic: floral prints, a locket, a lacy bra

> If I really
> want a little
> extra something to
> give myself more oomph, I
> don't argue with myself anymore
> about indulging that. I'll put on my
> more daring lipstick and wear it proudly.
>
> ERIN JANE AMABILE, MAGICAL FASHIONISTA

Integrate Your Sparkle

After that last section, you might be thinking: "Yeah, right, like I'm going to dress like a sex kitten for the parent/teacher conference or like an anarchist for my desk job." And that brings up a perfectly valid point. It might not be likely to match the mood of the day or to help you feel wonderful in your own skin if you were to wear a lacy short skirt and heels to meet with your child's teacher, or a nose ring to your conservative office job.

So, your assignment is twofold. First, find little ways to incorporate these aspects that do match the feeling of the day. To incorporate more sexiness at the parent/teacher conference, you might realize that you feel great wearing high-heeled sandals instead of flats. To the day job, you might discover that it's fun to wear a slightly edgy (yet still tasteful) cuff bracelet to honor your inner anarchist without ruffling any feathers.

And for the second part of the assignment, if you find that there are facets of you that you'd particularly like to embody but that don't currently have outlets in your daily life, ask yourself how you can find some. Perhaps your inner sex kitten would like to take a pole dancing class. And maybe your inner anarchist would like to organize a protest.

Gently push your boundaries in ways that feel daring and fun—but also somehow just right. You'll add depth and dimension not only to your look but also to your life, and each will nourish and enhance the other.

Confidence Charm

Hold a hematite crystal and five dried allspice berries in your open palm, and empower them in bright sunlight for at least one minute. Place them in a piece of red flannel and tie closed with hemp twine. Anoint with essential oil of cedar, jasmine, or cinnamon. Hold in both hands, close your eyes, and visualize/imagine/ feel yourself being utterly confident no matter where you are, whom you are with, or what you are doing. Invisibly safety-pin to the inside of your clothes as desired.

You Are Exactly Where You're Supposed to Be

Meditation Ritual for Extra Sparkle

You might do this ritual just before or after getting dressed for an occasion during which you'd like to shine.

Light a white candle and a stick of cinnamon or jasmine incense (or diffuse essential oil of cinnamon or jasmine). Sit comfortably, with your spine straight. Close your eyes and take some deep breaths as you consciously relax your body.

When you feel ready, cup your hands around the flame at a safe distance. Imagine the light and energy from the flame entering your hands as you say:

This is the divine light of charm and grace.
I recognize that this light is within me now.
As I acknowledge my own divinity,
my light and potency grow.

Now place one hand on your heart and one hand on your belly. Feel yourself imbibing and absorbing divine radiance. Then open your arms wide, as if you're about to embrace someone. Envision divine light coming down from the sky and entering the crown of your head, and also coming up from the core of the earth and entering through your tailbone, converging and endlessly radiating from your heart and hands. Say:

I am confident beyond measure.
My charm goes on for days.
My beauty knows no limits.
I am safe in my life and at home in my body.
I happily bless others with my divine radiance.

5

you are
A CELEBRATION

There is no such thing as "same old, same old." In fact, whether you're looking through the lens of astrology or astronomy, art or science, spirituality or practicality, no two days are alike.

For the purpose of going more deeply into how to enhance your personal energies and set positive conditions in motion via your wardrobe choices and self-care practices, this chapter will teach you about the planetary aspects that make each day unique. This way, you can align your intentions, moods, outfit, and accessories with the magical energies of the moment and flow harmoniously with the most auspicious aspects of the day.

But even more importantly, fashion is a vehicle for celebrating the day for its own sake. When we come into the moment to select an ensemble that feels right to us and accentuates our inner experience of beauty as well as our outer radiance, we are grounding ourselves in the true preciousness of the now.

Have you ever considered that a dress can be just as comfy as your grubbiest sweats? Or that a pair of jeans we look great in can be just as cozy as a pair of jeans we're not too crazy about? I know I've touched on this in previous chapters, but it bears repeating: even though some days you might genuinely feel like dressing simply and casually, make sure you don't make choices based on saving all the best stuff in your closet for a "special day." Today *is* a special day!

Days of the Week

A particular planet "rules" each day of the week, giving each day its own distinct vibration and energetic qualities. In fact, although I'm not religious about it, the day of the week (and its ruling planet) is one of the first things I take into account when deciding what to wear.

Even if you wear a uniform to work or otherwise don't have a lot of freedom with your wardrobe on any certain day, you can still incorporate an awareness of the day's planetary ruler into the colors and vibe of your lingerie (and possibly accessories) in order to mystically align with and benefit from the unique energies of the moment.

Monday is ruled by the moon. (Think "Moon-day.") As such, it possesses introspective, receptive, intuitive, dreamy, feminine, watery, and generally lunar qualities. On Mondays I scan my closet for colors such as black, white, cream, blue, lavender, silver, and purple. Depending on other aspects of the day (such as the moon sign—see page 89), I might be more likely to choose silver accessories rather than gold ones. I also might go for more of a flowy, watery look (see chapter 3's "Water Fashions"), and I'll consider wearing imagery that depicts the moon or that relates to the moon, such as a lotus flower or an owl. Patterns that match Monday include circles, crescents, wavy lines, and swirls. Gemstone choices might include moonstone and labradorite.

Tuesday is ruled by Mars. The energetic qualities that color the day include passion, power, aggression, assertiveness, confidence, leadership, and initiative. Tuesday sends me looking for pieces that appear in the ranges of red, black, or gray. And, generally speaking, I like to assemble outfits that support feelings of strength and empowerment. Bold patterns and colors, and larger jewelry, are likely to feel right on Tuesdays. Excellent gemstone choices might include garnet, ruby, and tiger's-eye.

Wednesday is ruled by Mercury. Mercury energy is swiftly moving and has to do with words, communication, and travel. Because Mercury energy is so changeable, I'm more likely to look at the moon sign when choosing my color, but grounded, welcoming colors such as yellow, purple, green, and brown are often nicely balancing choices for Wednesday. Airy colors—like grays and whites—can also work nicely. Wednesdays often seem to call for patterns and styles with a lighter, simpler feel. As for gemstones, you might consider agate, fluorite, or quartz.

Thursday is ruled by Jupiter. Jupiter is related to expansion and prosperity. On Thursdays I like to choose colors related to wealth and thriving: purple, green, turquoise, blue, or any shade of red (and often depending on the moon sign). When assembling my outfit and choosing my accessories, I like to keep in mind the word *luxury* in order to exude a feeling of wealth and maximize the wealth-drawing energies of the day. Sumptuous fabrics and outfits with a tailored, generally affluent look often feel right. Crystal accessories might include citrine quartz, aventurine, turquoise, or chrysocolla.

Friday is ruled by Venus. Friday is the day of love! Colors that are especially suited to align us with the energy of the day include pink, red, coral, peach, lavender, purple, white, and cream. You might also like to consider romantic styles and imagery: ruffles, flowers, hearts, and such (or whatever may fall into your personal romantic range). In other words, what would the hero or heroine of your ideal love story be wearing if he or she were having a similar day to the one you have planned? Wear that. Romantic gemstone choices might include such things as rose quartz, lepidolite, rhodocrosite, or watermelon tourmaline.

Saturday is ruled by Saturn. Saturn is commonly known as "the planet of limitation." This is not at all a bad thing: limits and boundaries are truly imperative when it comes to protection, safety, and emotional well-being. Saturdays are also associated with completing projects and bringing cycles to a close. I find Saturday energy to feel very comfortable, safe, and down-to-earth. I often choose to wear grounding colors such as black, gray, and brown. I also have a Saturn charm necklace that I really like to wear. Simple styles and patterns, and things on the comfier side, might feel good to you today. Gemstones that would be particularly auspicious would include obsidian, hematite, and pyrite.

Sunday is ruled by the sun. This makes Sundays especially in alignment with the fire element as well as health, healing, brightness, happiness, and simplicity. On Sundays I like to wear colors evocative of light and fire such as red, yellow, orange, white, and cream. I also like to wear gold jewelry and accents. Wardrobe choices related to the fire element, like sparkles, animal prints, a lot of different colors, zig-zags, star shapes, and sun shapes (also see chapter 3's "Fire Fashions") are great, although sometimes just something white or pale yellow with gold jewelry might feel sunshiny in exactly the right way. Crystals of the day are things such as fire opal, sunstone, amber, and topaz.

Moon Signs

The moon sign, which changes every couple of days or so, also lends its own energetic chords to the song of time. In addition to looking at the moon sign to help determine what to wear, I look at it to get an idea of the flavor of the day: it noticeably colors our moods, intentions, and the ways that we perceive and interact with the world. That's why, each year, I get a calendar that reveals the day's moon sign, such as *Llewellyn's Astrological Calendar*. Astrological almanacs or day planners are also great ways to stay current on the moon sign, or you can easily discover the moon sign online at a site such as www.lunarium.co.uk.

When the moon is in Aries, the spirit of the day will likely be enthusiastic, energized, and friendly, like a happy baby or a puppy dog. Intentions that fit with Aries moon energy include starting new things, making or maintaining friendships, and having fun. The element associated with this moon sign is fire and the planet associated with this moon sign is Mars, so when considering color choices (also keeping in mind the day of the week), you might like to lean toward red, gold, yellow, cream, or white.

When the moon is in Taurus, the spirit of the day will likely be sensual or passionately resolute, like the heroine of an Italian romance or an action hero. Intentions that fit with Taurus moon energy include sticking to things for the long haul, career success, and manifesting anything into the physical realm, such as finances, resources, or a new place to live. The element associated with this moon sign is earth and the planet associated with this moon sign is Venus, so when considering color choices (also keeping in mind the day of the week), you might like to lean toward brown, yellow, gold, red, terra cotta, pink, brownish purple, or cream.

When the moon is in Gemini, the spirit of the day will likely be playful, thought-and-word oriented, and changeable, like a wistfully windy day that keeps alternating between sun, clouds, rain, and rainbows. Intentions that fit with the Gemini moon include scintillating conversations, writing, playing, and creativity. The element associated with this moon sign is air and the planet associated with this moon sign is Mercury, so when considering color choices (also keeping in mind the day of the week), you might like to lean toward white, yellow, cream, silver, gray, lavender, pale or bright blue, pink, green, and all pastels.

When the moon is in Cancer, the spirit of the day will likely be nurturing, soft-spoken, receptive, and home/family oriented, like a doting parent. Intentions that fit with the Cancer moon include mothering and caretaking, preparing and serving food, allowing oneself to receive (e.g., love or resources), relaxation, self-care, and creating a cozy atmosphere in the home. The element associated with this moon sign is water and the (astrological) planet associated with this moon sign is the moon, so when considering color choices (also keeping in mind the day of the week), you might like to lean toward black, white, cream, silver, purple, lavender, and deep blue.

When the moon is in Leo, the spirit of the day will likely be extroverted and social, like a Hollywood starlet on the red carpet. Intentions that fit with the Leo moon include performing, public speaking, socializing, and generally shining one's light in the world. The element associated with this moon sign is fire and the (astrological) planet associated with this moon sign is the sun, so when considering color choices (also keeping in mind the day of the week), you might like to lean toward red, burgundy, orange, bright yellow, gold, cream, or white.

When the moon is in Virgo, the spirit of the day will likely be clean, ordered, and health-oriented, like an upscale day spa. Intentions that fit with the Virgo moon include exercise, organization, self-improvement, nutrition, analysis, cleansing, and cleaning. The element associated with this moon sign is earth and the planet associated with this moon sign is Mercury, so when considering color choices (also keeping in mind the day of the week), you might like to lean toward white, cream, brown, tan, yellow, gray, or navy blue.

When the moon is in Libra, the spirit of the day will likely be balanced, harmonious, and beautifying, like a bouquet of lilacs and a clean white tablecloth on a table set for two. Intentions that fit with the Libra moon include love, romance, fairness, balance, harmony, order, and beautification. The element associated with this moon sign is air and the planet associated with this moon sign is Venus, so when considering color choices (also keeping in mind the day of the week), you might like to lean toward white, cream, gray, pink, silver, lavender, or purple.

When the moon is in Scorpio, the spirit of the day will likely be sexual, charismatic, and secretive, like an undercover agent or a cult leader. Intentions that fit with the Scorpio moon include sexuality, charisma, artistic passion/ appreciation, spirituality, creativity, and rebirth. The element associated with this moon sign is water and the planet associated with this moon sign is Pluto, so when considering color choices (also keeping in mind the day of the week), you might like to lean toward black, deep blue, indigo, gray, turquoise, or white.

When the moon is in Sagittarius, the spirit of the day will likely be expansive, fun, friendly, and adventurous, like a trip to Paris with your best girlfriend or an exploratory romp in the woods. Intentions that fit with the Sagittarius moon include travel, wealth, adventures, socializing, playfulness, and friendship. The element associated with this moon sign is fire and the planet associated with this moon sign is Jupiter, so when considering color choices (also keeping in mind the day of the week), you might like to lean toward red, warm purple, gold, green, turquoise, or white.

When the moon is in Capricorn, the spirit of the day will likely be driven, focused, and success-oriented, like a solitary hike to the top of a mountain. Intentions that fit with the Capricorn moon include career success, excellence, determination, and will. The element associated with this moon sign is earth and the planet associated with this moon sign is Saturn, so when considering color choices (also keeping in mind the day of the week), you might like to lean toward gray, black, brown, white, or cream.

When the moon is in Aquarius, the spirit of the day will likely be philosophical, offbeat, artistic, humanitarian, and erudite, like the president of the debate club or a founder of a nonprofit organization. Intentions that fit with the Aquarius moon include air travel, intellectual pursuits, debates, art, and humanitarian efforts. The element associated with this moon sign is air and the planet associated with this moon sign is Uranus, so when considering color choices (also keeping in mind the day of the week), you might like to lean toward silver, white, cream, lavender, bright or light blue, or gray.

When the moon is in Pisces, the spirit of the day will likely be dreamy, watery, and intuitive, like a mermaid or Luna Lovegood (in Harry Potter). Intentions that fit with the Pisces moon include intuition, emotional connection, sleep, and peace. The element associated with this moon sign is water and the planet associated with this moon sign is Neptune, so when considering color choices (also keeping in mind the day of the week), you might like to lean toward black, deep blue, bright blue, white, cream, silver, or gray.

⟨⟩ Fashion Icons of the Zodiac ⟨⟩

The iconic examples of each astrological sign below can help you get an idea of the fashion flavor of the day as determined by the day's moon sign. Additionally, as mentioned in chapter 3, our sun signs have a lot to do with how we shine our light in the world, so you might also keep this in mind as you discover your astrological siblings below.

Aries: *Sarah Jessica Parker, Diana Ross*

Taurus: *Audrey Hepburn, Uma Thurman*

Gemini: *Nicole Kidman, Marilyn Monroe*

Cancer: *Meryl Streep, Frida Kahlo*

Leo: *Mick Jagger, Madonna*

Virgo: *Greta Garbo, Lauren Bacall*

Libra: *Brigitte Bardot, Donna Karan*

Scorpio: *Julia Roberts, Grace Slick*

Sagittarius: *Bette Midler, Tyra Banks*

Capricorn: *Marlene Dietrich, Kate Moss*

Aquarius: *Yoko Ono, Oprah*

Pisces: *Drew Barrymore, Elizabeth Taylor*

Phases of the Moon

When we walk the path of the magical fashionista, we live in intimate synchronicity with our dreams, goals, and desires. We don't just approach our closet or our self-care efforts mindlessly or haphazardly; rather, all our actions (including choosing our clothes and accessories) are opportunities to focus our intentions and express love for ourselves and the world.

When you begin to live this way on a regular basis, you will find it exceptionally helpful to pay attention to the phases of the moon.

The day of the new moon is a day of new beginnings. A fresh cycle has started. We might plant seeds for new intentions or projects.

The period between the new moon and the full moon (as the moon is waxing) is a period of growth. It's a time to pay attention to the nourishment and expansion of our goals, desires, wealth, and resources. The waxing moon calls us to focus on manifesting, magnetizing, and drawing things in.

The day of the full moon is a moment of fruition and fullness. The energy of the day is heightened and potent: it's a great time to fuel intentions with power. And, because the energy is at its pinnacle and is about to begin waning, it can also be a great time to set the intention to release things and conditions that we no longer need.

The period between the full moon and the dark moon (as the moon is waning) is a period of cleansing, releasing, and diminishing. During this time we have more success letting go of what we no longer need, such as extra pounds, challenging health conditions, clutter, and limiting beliefs.

The day of the dark moon (the day before the new moon) is a period of rest. The cycle is at its ebb. It can be a great day to relax, clear your mind, take inventory of your present situation, and clear the decks for the fresh cycle to start.

If this is all new to you, it might seem like a lot of extra stuff to worry about, but it doesn't have to be that way. I suggest leisurely taking a look at the day of the week and the day's moon sign once a day, just to make a note of it. Also, as you glance at a new calendar month, take a look at where the new and the full moons fall. And, whenever you think of it, gaze up into the sky and see if you can find the moon. Notice where it is and how big it is. In time, just like inhaling and exhaling, it will become second nature to know whether the moon is waxing or waning, and you'll begin to fall into a naturally more harmonious life rhythm.

There's no need to force any of this—you can let it be a natural progression. Take it nice and easy all the way. After all, most of the people we're descended from—like 99.9 percent of them!—were intimately connected with the phases of the moon, so it's in your DNA.

Celebrate the Wheel of the Year

Of course we all know that fashions and conventions change with the seasons: e.g., fall colors, spring collections, and winter hats. But when you begin to see fashion as an opportunity to honor your divinity and celebrate the day, you'll realize that choosing colors and styles that mirror the seasons can also be a beautiful way to stay awake to the freshness of the moment. What's more, for most of the time that humans have been present on this planet, we've been much more in touch with the elements and the entire natural world than we are today. When we connect with the vibe of the season—and tune in to things like the autumn leaves, the sparkling snow, or the tiny purple wildflowers showing up in the grass—and then honor this vibe with our clothing choices, we are restoring some of our natural synchronization with the world around us. When it comes to our happiness, physical health, and degree of inspiration, this can't help but reap amazing benefits.

Of course we all know about the more mainstream holidays, but there is a slightly more ancient (and organic) collection of holidays that magical and metaphysical folk of the present day still celebrate that is aligned with the harvest cycle and the cycles of the sun and moon. Here you'll find brief descriptions of these ancient holidays, along with some general wardrobe suggestions for each.

Samhain/Halloween

This holiday was often celebrated, and is still celebrated by many, as a day of purification. The smoke of bonfires cleansed and refreshed the community while warming them and fortifying their spirits before the darkest, coldest time of the year arrived. Additionally, in cultures all over the globe, this is considered to be the time of the year when the "veil between the worlds" of the living and the dead is the thinnest. For the *Dia de los Muertos* festival, for example, people assemble altars to honor their deceased loved ones.

> **Colors:** *black, white, gray, purple, orange*
>
> **Styles:** *gauzy, gothic, dark*
>
> **Crystals:** *opal, moonstone, obsidian, labradorite*
>
> **Scents:** *copal, palo santo*

Winter Solstice/Yule

DECEMBER 20–22 (CHECK CALENDAR FOR PRECISE DAY)

A precursor to Christmas, this is the time when the days are shortest, the sun is lowest, and the earth's axis is farthest from the sun. Simultaneously, however, it is the moment when this darkness begins to ebb as the cycle turns once again to move toward springtime. In other words, it is the (re)birth of the sun. Hence, it is a celebration welcoming warmth and light. It is a time to honor expansion, wealth, generosity, family, and friends.

Colors: *red, white, green, purple, blue*

Styles: *cozy, warm, festive, traditional*

Crystals: *bloodstone, sunstone, star sapphire, gold*

Scents: *cinnamon, clove, frankincense*

Chinese or Lunar New Year
JANUARY 21–FEBRUARY 20 (CHECK CALENDAR)

This is the time when the Chinese astrological cycle begins anew. It's celebrated with firecrackers to cleanse away the challenges of the old year and welcome in a beautiful new one. Dragons are also a common symbol for this celebration, as they're considered very fortunate. It's a good idea to make a note of the sign of the year, as well as the element associated with the year, and to read up on what that means from an astrological perspective, as this day marks a definite energetic shift.

Colors: *red, black, blue, green*

Styles: *festive (you might want to incorporate the element associated with the New Year into your outfit; see chapter 3's "Chinese Astrology and You")*

Crystals: *jade, moonstone, white quartz*

Scents: *sunflower, narcissus*

Imbolc/Candlemas

FEBRUARY 1–2

A fire celebration and a day dedicated to the fiery Celtic goddess Brighid, this is a time to celebrate the quickening before springtime and the returning of warmth and the sun. It's a day for cleansing, healing, protecting, and calling in blessings of all kinds. Perhaps light a red candle while you're getting dressed and preparing for the day.

> **Colors:** *red, burgundy, white*
>
> **Styles:** *cheerful, bright, clean*
>
> **Crystals:** *ruby, garnet*
>
> **Scents:** *orange, lemon, vanilla, floral*

Ostara/Vernal Equinox

MARCH 20–23 (CHECK CALENDAR)

Today we celebrate the springtime and fertility goddess Ostara, after whom Easter is named. It's no coincidence that she's associated with eggs and that she often appears with a giant white bunny. As you may imagine, this is a day to plant seeds for the future and to celebrate the still-increasing fertility and warmth of the season.

> **Colors:** *white, yellow, pastels*
>
> **Styles:** *fresh, cheerful, springy*
>
> **Crystals:** *egg-shaped crystals of all varieties*
>
> **Scents:** *narcissus, rose, floral*

Beltane

Possibly named after the Celtic sun god Belenus, whose name translates to "bright and shining one," Beltane is an observance of the beginning of the summery months. A celebration of fertility, flowers, and all things green and growing, and a particularly vibrant and empowering time of the year, this is also a time when bonfires were traditionally burned to cleanse and energize the festival participants. Additionally, Maypoles (a powerful fertility symbol) were—and still are—danced around and adorned.

> **Colors:** *white, pink, green, blue, yellow, brights and pastels*
>
> **Styles:** *celebratory, floral, sensual, romantic*
>
> **Crystals:** *moss agate, watermelon tourmaline, lapis lazuli, emerald*
>
> **Scents:** *lilac, honeysuckle, rose*

Summer Solstice/Midsummer

JUNE 20–23 (CHECK CALENDAR)

Just as the Winter Solstice marks the birth of the sun, the Summer Solstice is the time that marks the decline of the sun and the coming of the dark time of the year. This is the yin contained within the yang, however, as this is also the time when the days are longest and the sun is highest in the sky. According to author Ellen Dugan, this summery, balmy time is also "the best night of the year to commune with the elemental kingdom and the fairies."

Colors: *green, yellow, blue*

Styles: *light, summery, beachy, celebratory*

Crystals: *lepidolite, selenite, sodalite, seashells*

Scents: *ylang ylang, neroli, orange*

Lughnasadh/Lammas
AUGUST 1

Another fire festival, today celebrates the early harvest time. Named after Lugh, the Celtic deity of healing and light, it's associated with healing, music, fertility, divination, and abundance.

Colors: *yellow, orange, brown*

Styles: *peasant, hippie, relaxed*

Crystals: *topaz, citrine quartz, agate, jasper*

Scents: *sunflower, sandalwood, gardenia*

Mabon/Autumn Equinox
SEPTEMBER 20–23 (CHECK CALENDAR)

A period associated with one of my favorite goddesses, Demeter, her daughter Persephone, and the myth associated with the two, this is the time of the year that has to do with the harvest, the reaping, and the coming dark time of the year. As such, it has connotations related to both abundance and death. The Demeter/Persephone myth was the framework for the Eleusinian Mysteries, a closely guarded secret ritual practiced for centuries in ancient Greece. Like Mabon itself, this ritual was believed to have something to do with both the harvest season and the perpetual cycle of birth, life, death, and rebirth.

Colors: *yellow, gold, orange, brown, black*

Styles: *dramatic, whimsical, earthy*

Crystals: *carnelian, jasper, onyx, chrysocolla*

Scents: *frankincense, myrrh, patchouli*

6

you are
A MAGICIAN

At this point, you're probably starting to get the picture that your entire wardrobe and all your accessories have the potential to serve as a grand magical toolbox: a set of beloved and beautiful items that collectively adorn and enhance both your physical body and your experience of life. So true!

This chapter is about getting even deeper into the magic: zeroing in on your intentions, then utilizing your wardrobe to help manifest those intentions in specific ways. Additionally, you'll learn more about how you can employ the unseen world (your thoughts, feelings, and intentions, as well as divine and otherworldly beings) to accentuate the seen world (your wardrobe, accessories, and general appearance).

But first, if you feel so inclined, this might be an excellent time to perform a blessing on your entire closet. You might

> Our
> desire to wear
> clothing first emerged
> not because we felt
> shame…or were cold…
> but because clothes were
> seen as magical.
>
> TIM GUNN, AUTHOR
> AND FASHION EXPERT

choose a specific intention to activate or choose a bunch. For example, intentions might include increasing your abundance, enhancing your attractiveness, or intensifying your personal magnetism.

Then, in the future, you can bless your closet periodically, after you clear clutter and organize or whenever you feel inspired.

Here's an all-purpose closet blessing ritual that incorporates all three of the intentions mentioned in the example above:

After clearing and organizing your closet (see chapter 1), light a stick of sandalwood incense and place it in a holder. Use it to safely smudge the inside of your closet, and then set it at the bottom of your closet in a safe place where it definitely won't light anything on fire. Then close your closet doors. Place your palms on the outside of the doors and say:

> With the freshness of the new moon,
>
> With the divine sweetness of sandalwood,
>
> And with all the love that is in my heart,
>
> I now bless this wardrobe with love.
>
> May it enhance my beauty.
>
> May it fuel the potency of my
> unique and beautiful essence.
>
> May it help magnetize prosperity,
> love, and all good things.
>
> In all ways, may it serve me well.
>
> Thank you, thank you, thank you.
> Blessed be. And so it is.

Allow the incense to burn all the way down.

Vestments of Power

In the book *Secrets and Mysteries,* author Denise Linn suggests designating a key piece in your wardrobe, such as a wrap, scarf, or shawl, as a "vestment of power." To imbue it with energy, she further suggests, you might engage in practices such as saying prayers over it, sewing crystals into it, or anointing it with essential oils. Then you can wear it whenever you'd like an extra feeling of confidence, personal power, and divine support.

Along similar lines, I'd like to suggest that with any outfit—on any given day or for any given purpose—you

I will often dress like a goddess whose energy or essence I'm hoping to invoke for certain situations. If I feel that I need assistance from Isis, for example, I'll wear all gold jewelry and generally black and golden-toned things. Or sometimes I will want to invoke Aphrodite's loving and sensual presence, so I'll dress in more aqua tones and sweet pinks and whites, or lacy things. And the same with Lakshmi! To invoke a feeling of abundance and affluence, I'll dress in a more eastern Indian style and wear her colors of pink and green.

SEDONA SOULFIRE,
SACRED DANCER AND PRIESTESS

might choose a particular piece that feels powerful to you (accessory, garment, or undergarment) and infuse it with the intention and energy to serve as a magical charm. Bellow, you'll find a nice little collection of ideas for how to do this—but please do not feel limited by them! The sky is the limit when it comes to concocting blessings for your wardrobe. Just keep in mind that phrasing things in the positive ("thank you for my abundant wealth") rather than the negative ("Thank you for helping me to stop experiencing financial challenges") is much more powerful. Also remember that strong belief in a positive outcome, as well as a visualization and expectation of success, are important ingredients when it comes to manifesting your desires.

A Lingerie Glamour Charm

A "glamour charm" might be defined as a specific, magically infused object that shrouds you in a veil of magnetic beauty and attractiveness.

According to the author Helena Frith-Powell, in France lingerie stores are much more of a thing than in England and America, and part of French women's irresistible mystique comes from the fact that they pay a great deal of attention to how beautiful they look without their outer clothes on every single day. Knowing their lingerie looks fabulous and feeling particularly delectable garments on their bare skin naturally lends a subtle yet very real dimension to their outer attractiveness.

On a Friday, choose an especially lovely and beloved bra or pair of panties (or, if you want to be really French, a matching bra and panties set). Spread them on a table or dresser top, place a pink candle in a holder, and then place the holder (safely) near the lingerie and light it. Direct your palms toward the assemblage as you visualize the panties imbued with golden-pink light. Say:

> **As I wear this lovely lingerie, I exude an**
> **aura of sensuality and magnetic charm. I**
> **drink deeply of the bliss in each moment and**
> **experience all of life as a delectable treat.**

Close your eyes and feel a deep, earthy joy in simply being present in your physical body. See yourself carrying this feeling throughout your day. Extinguish the candle and put on the lingerie.

Pants:
What Are You Grounded In?

Because pants clothe almost our entire lower body, they're an especially good garment to choose when you want to feel really grounded and rooted in your magical purpose. They also possess an aura of masculinity (since they have only been worn by women in our culture relatively recently), determination and authority (as in the phrase "wears the pants"), intuition (as in the phrase "flying by the seat of my pants"), and affluence (as in the phrase "fancy pants").

Wear the Pants: An Authority Ritual

Are you stepping into a new role as an authority figure of some kind, or are you preparing for a certain occasion when you will be the boss? Or perhaps you would like to shift the balance of power in a particular situation or relationship so that you have the upper hand; this may be the ritual for you.

When the moon is full, just before sunrise, take a pair of pants outside that have been carefully selected with the goal of authority in mind—i.e., make sure they make you feel like a boss or at least feel comfortable being bossy. You can also do this inside if necessary. Lay them on a table or blanket and set a candleholder on top containing a red candle (set a book below it if you need to steady it). As the sun rises, face east and chant the following words toward the pants, mentally directing the energy of the sunrise, candle, and words into them. Imagine the words being imbued within the weave of the fabric itself.

I am the master of all that I see,

Everyone listens and answers to me,

Graceful and fair as I unite all toward our goal,

With honor and wisdom I step into my role.

By the Seat of Your Pants: An Intuition Ritual

Perhaps you're about to embark upon a day when the only way you can possibly prepare is by getting in alignment with your intuition. What will happen exactly? What will the interviewer ask? What questions will be on the test? Beyond general expectations, there is no way to know precisely. You'll have to fly by the seat of your pants.

Find or create a cute patch depicting wings: angel wings, butterfly wings, fairy wings, airplane wings, or bird wings (whatever feels powerful to you). Then, with thread that is

the same color as the pants, sew it into the inside of the
seat, preferably so that the stitches are not visible from
the outside. When this is complete, hold the pants in both
hands and say:

My intuition is activated!

**I am in my element when I am
flying by the seat of my pants!**

Wherever I need to fly, I can fly!

Whatever I need to do, I can do!

**I am safe, I am smart, and I am in the right
place at the right time doing the right thing.**

**All doors are open to me, and I fly
through them with ease. All is well.**

Fancy Pants: An Abundance Ritual

On a Thursday during a waxing moon, choose a freshly
washed, attractive pair of pants that feel abundant to you
(they don't have to actually be expensive, but it's ideal if
they at least look that way) and hang them on a hanger.
Light a stick of cinnamon or patchouli incense and safely
smudge the pants with the smoke, being careful to catch
any burning embers with an incense holder or dish. As you
smudge them, say:

**Goddess Lakshmi and divine light of
endless abundance, please bless these
pants with your prosperous flow.**

**As I wear them, may I receive a continuous
shower of luxurious blessings.**

> May avalanches and windfalls of
> wealth appear at every turn.
>
> My I embrace and exude the fanciness
> that is my natural state.
>
> **Thank you!**

Visualize a flow of energy like a sparkling stream containing flecks of green and gold light filling and surrounding the pants. Then put them on and see this magnetic flow of energy completely filling and surrounding your aura as well.

Shirts, Blouses, and Tanks: The Message You're Sending

What are you wearing on top? This is what will show up in most photos and will likely be the thing that others will most clearly remember about your outfit. It accentuates your face and lies on top of your emotional centers: your belly and heart. Even if it doesn't profess an actual verbal message (such as "I heart LA"), you might think of it as the flag you are flying—the message you are sending to the world. (See the "You Are a Guru" chapter for color and symbol charts that reveal specific magical energies.)

Notice Me and Remember Me: Top Spell I

When I was in acting school (if you will recall, I was once an acting student and aspiring movie star), some teachers used to say that you should wear something memorable to auditions so that you would stand out from the crowd. This ritual draws upon the same concept. Use it for an audition, an interview, or anytime you want to stand out and be remembered.

Choose a top that is memorable without being garish or costumey (unless, for some reason, that's desirable for the situation). For example, perhaps it's made of a sumptuous material or is shimmery or boldly colored. When the moon is waxing and in the sign of Leo, Aries, or Sagittarius, at noon on a clear and sunny day (granted, you might have to plan ahead or wait a bit for these conditions to coincide), take it outside and lay it out on a pure white cloth in the full light of the sun. Place a white quartz crystal in the center of it, approximately where your heart chakra would be (the center of your sternum). Without letting your shadow pass over it, aim your palms toward the shirt. Direct the energy of your words into the shirt as you chant:

> **Shining bright, I catch your eye.**
> **Shining bright, I stick in your mind.**
> **Shining bright, I steal the show.**
> **Who am I? What am I all about?**
> **Wouldn't you like to know!**
> *(Then whisper your first and last name three times.)*

Bring the shirt inside and keep the crystal point near it until the full moon. Then wear the shirt, and enjoy the magic, whenever the situation calls for it.

Trust Me and Respect Me: Top Spell II

But maybe you don't need to stand out from the crowd—maybe you just need to appear as trustworthy as you actually are. For example, perhaps you're running for office, selling used cars, or being interviewed for a job with a high degree of responsibility. If this is the case, you might like to charm your (solidly responsible-looking) shirt in the following way.

When the full, or somewhat close-to-full, moon is in Capricorn, Virgo, or Taurus, at midnight, lay the shirt flat (on a table, bed, or cloth on the floor). Light four white candles and place them at the cardinal points surrounding the shirt (use a compass or just estimate). Place a solid, slightly large rock or gemstone in the center of the shirt, roughly where your heart chakra would be (in the center of your sternum). Say:

Solid as a rock,

Deserving of respect,

Stalwart, loyal, wise, and true,

Worthy of the utmost trust.

*(Confidently chant your first and
last name three times.)*

Extinguish the candles, remove the rock, and hang the shirt in your closet. Wear it whenever you'd like to inspire trust, and be sure to live up to the aura you emanate (otherwise your karma will get wonky).

Love Me and Lavish Gifts Upon Me: Top Spell III

We are all deserving of love. What's more, since others are a vehicle through which the universe lavishes gifts upon us, you might think of it as a virtue to be able to gracefully receive. (See, this ritual isn't as self-serving as it seems!)

Choose an attractive and lovable top. On a Friday when the moon is waxing, spread the shirt on a pink or red cloth, then strew the petals of six pink roses over the top. Direct your palms toward the shirt as you say:

I am loved and lovable.

**I am a magnet for all forms
of lavish abundance.**

**Gifts of all sorts find their way
into my possession.**

**I gracefully receive, bringing joy both
to me and to the givers of the gifts.**

**I am the beloved child of a loving
and abundant universe.**

Thank you, thank you, thank you.

Leave the shirt under the petals overnight. Awake before sunrise. Take the shirt outside (or stay inside if necessary), and as the sun rises over the horizon, mist the shirt lightly with rose water. Hang it in your closet, and wear it whenever you'd especially like to attract love and gifts of love.

Skirts and Dresses:
All Kinds of Feminine

A stick figure in a skirt is the universal symbol for the ladies' room, a slang term for a woman is "skirt," and very few manly men are generally found in them (Scottish traditionalists excluded, although kilts aren't technically skirts). Rather than limiting us to one view of what it means to be girly, however, dresses and skirts run the gamut of femininity—from flouncy and romantic to sleek and businesslike.

Skirting the Issue:
Putting Your Feminine Wiles to Use

I grew up in California during the late seventies and all of the eighties, and my mom was of the hippie persuasion, so I wasn't raised to believe that using one's feminine wiles was a good thing. However, now that I've investigated the issue for myself, I have come to a different conclusion and feel that there's no reason to throw the baby out with the bath water.

If you're a feminine sort, you've probably already discovered that your soft, sweet attractiveness can help you in a number of situations. This ritual can help you channel that power even more effectively.

Choose a skirt in which you feel especially girly or feminine and especially attractive. On a Friday when the moon is in Cancer, Scorpio, or Pisces, hang it on a hanger. Light two sticks each of rose, sandalwood, and vanilla incense, and hold them together in a bundle as you smudge the skirt with the smoke and chant:

You Are a Magician

Goddesslike yet soft,

Radiating beauty like the sun and
yet receptive like the moon,

I now activate my innate female power.

I happily allow my bewitching
smile and natural sparkle

To magnetize all forms of
blessings and success.

Extinguish all but one stick of rose incense and allow it to safely burn all the way down near the skirt. (Feel free to save the other sticks for future use.)

Wear the skirt when your feminine wiles will come in especially handy, whenever your femininity could use a boost, or when it just seems fun to be girly.

The Belle of the Ball: Enchanting a Dress for a Special Day

For women—generally speaking—when the occasion is especially special, it usually demands a dress. From weddings to award ceremonies to grand galas, the following ritual has got you covered.

Take your time and find the perfect dress. You'll know it when you try it on. Then, no more than three days before the event, hang it on a hanger and suspend it where you can see it in the room. Create a garland/pendant/sash-type thing with hemp twine and at least three rose blossoms. Choose any combination of the following: red for passion, pink for romance or friendship, and white for pure and simple beauty and positivity. Add other flowers according to their symbolism as desired (for inspiration, see my book *The Magic of Flowers*). Also add a bell (please be sure to cleanse it for at least a minute or two by bathing it in sage smoke or the light of the sun) and a small star charm (cleansed in the same way). Get as creative as you like with this garland or keep it on the simple side.

Hang the garland on the hanger as well, draped over the dress in an attractive way. Then mist the dress lightly with rose water into which you've added a few drops of sandalwood essential oil. (Go without the oil if you're worried it might stain.) Say:

> **Radiant, joyful, magnetic, and blessed,**
>
> **I generously shine my beautiful light.**
>
> **I am the belle of the ball and**
> **the star of the show,**
>
> **and everything goes my way.**

Direct as much positivity toward the dress as you can, and then say:

> **Thank you, thank you, thank you.**
>
> **Blessed be. And so it is.**

Leave the garland on the dress until the event, and then, within one moon cycle, release the flowers in a moving body of water or near the base of a tree. Keep the bell and star charms as keepsakes, give them to a younger relative, or reuse them in another ritual. You might also like to conceal them in your purse on the day of the event to add even more oomph. If it works with the dress, you can also tie them into a piece of fabric and safety-pin them to the inside of your bra.

Jackets and Coats:
Wrapped in Magic

Like Gandalf's cloak, Philip Marlowe's trench coat, or your grandma's crocheted shawl, outer wraps can define your essence and artfully veil you in a particular energetic flavor.

Hippie Cloak Smoke: A Mystical Veil

You know who you are: you feel at home in the woods near a campfire drum circle or on a misty mountaintop reading *The Mists of Avalon* or the Lord of the Rings trilogy. Even if you're a city hippie, your aesthetic still leans toward the natural and the mystical. So of course you need a cloak, especially one that emanates a magical, peaceful vibe and lends luck and positivity to your circumstances.

At midnight, light a patchouli-scented candle and a bundle of dried white sage. While holding the sage bundle (and holding a small dish underneath to catch any burning embers), move it so that the smoke bathes and surrounds your hanging jacket, shawl, or cloak. As you do so, chant:

I am cloaked in a veil of magic,

I am swaddled in a veil of peace.

Extinguish the sage. Call on any angelic or otherworldly helpers that you'd like to bless the cloak, and ask them to do so. Thank them, then extinguish the candle. Optionally, anoint the cloak with patchouli and/or sage essential oil after the ritual, and periodically thereafter, to refresh the magic.

Gumshoe Ninja: Veil of Invisibility

My mom and I used to sit on a bridge over a canal way out on the edge of our small farm town and practice what we called "Ninja invisibility" at the rare times that a car or pickup truck would pass us. To do so, we simply imagined ourselves to be transparent, and then we got a kick out of the drivers appearing not to notice us.

While our invisibility experiments were recreational, there are times when it would be ideal not to be noticed: when you're a private investigator, for example—or, you know, if you have another really valid reason to be sneaking around.

Choose a coat that will help you blend into your surroundings or feel as inconspicuous as possible. Empower two small iron pyrite crystals in bright sunlight for at least a minute or two, then place one in each pocket. If there are no pockets, tie them in fabric and safety-pin them to the inside. If, however, you foresee metal detectors or friskings, omit the pyrite and safety pins, and simply anoint each side of your coat (perhaps near the pockets or shoulders) very lightly with burdock essential oil.

At midnight when the moon is in Scorpio, spread the coat on a black cloth and cover it with another black cloth (or just use the same one by folding it inside of the cloth). Light a black candle. Direct your palms toward the coat as you chant:

Invisible, invisible, invisible, invisible

Invisible, invisible, invisible, invisible.

No one notices, no one sees.

No one knows, no one wonders.

Under the radar, under the
radar, under the radar.

Envision yourself being completely transparent as you wear the coat and traverse the situation. Extinguish the candle. Hang the coat in your closet, and wear it as needed.

Bombshell Beauty: Veil of Elegance

Sometimes you find a coat that feels so elegant and so right. When you wear it, you feel like a movie star, and everything seems to go your way. If you've found that coat, this ritual will help you hone that glamorous mojo so that the coat veritably sings with elegance while also enhancing your beauty and intensifying your magical power.

If you already have a scent that you love and that feels right for the following purpose, use that. Otherwise, take your time and find a glamorous scent that helps you feel grounded in your own sensual beauty. (See the "You Are a Guru" chapter for guidance and ideas.) If the coat has a particular feeling—say, black-and-white movie star or modern-day royalty—find a scent that is aligned with that feeling.

Then, when the moon is full (or up to four days before full) and is in the sign of Libra or Taurus, at midnight, light a deep red candle and spray or anoint the coat with the perfume. Slip a tiny white quartz crystal into the pocket or sew it into the interior. Hold it in both hands and conjure up the feeling you'd like to feel while wearing that coat. Visualize experiences you'd like to have while wearing it or conditions you'd like to manifest, and feel as if they're already true. Say:

Goddess Venus, I call on you!

Please bless this coat with your irresistible glamour and beautiful magnetic light.

Thank you!

Extinguish the candle. Wear as desired.

Shoes:
Your Foundation

The word *understand* is reminiscent of feet. Indeed, the author and metaphysical pioneer Louise Hay says that feet represent "our understanding—of ourselves, of life, of others." (Consider how the phrase "walk a mile in another's shoes" denotes gaining a more intimate understanding of another's situation.) What's more, our feet are where we connect most essentially with Mother Earth. And when we're wearing shoes, they are our literal foundation.

With all this in mind, shoes—perhaps more than any other clothing item or accessory—set the tone for the rest of our ensemble, even for our day. They are an indication, or symbol, of the way we interact with and understand the world around us. No wonder we're so obsessed with them! (And no wonder Louboutin has had such success with his red soles—an added jolt of grounded power for sure!)

Walking on Sunshine: Shoe Spell I

For this basic spell, simply empower your shoes in the light of the noonday sun for at least five minutes. This will add a spring to your step whenever you wear them, and it will give your mood a joyful boost. Refresh the magic as desired.

Worship the Ground You Walk On: Shoe Spell II

I heard the Reverend Michael Beckwith (of Agape) speak about being aware that the ground you walk on is sacred simply because you walk on it. I love this idea of reminding ourselves that we are divine beings, and that the simple fact of our presence confers sacredness on our surroundings. One excellent way to do this would be to bless our shoes, keeping in mind all the while that they are the shoes of a divinity. Then, whenever we wear them, we'll have an added reminder that we are divine, and we will interact with the world as such.

On a Sunday morning, fill and surround your shoes with white rose blossoms. You can place them on a table or leave them on the ground, but make them into a little shoe altar. Place a white candle nearby (put it in a tall jar if you have cats), and light it. Optionally, light some frankincense, cedarwood, or sandalwood incense too. Visualize the shoes filled and surrounded by a sphere of blindingly bright, golden-white light, like a little sun. After an hour or so, extinguish the candle. Leave the shoes with the blossoms until the following morning, then wear as desired. (Dispose of the blossoms in a compost heap, running water, or at the base of a tree.)

These Boots Were Made for Walking: Shoe Spell III

Once, in the nineties, I put on a new (to me) pair of combat boots and then promptly went out in public and got into a loud argument with a stranger. I blame the boots. While this was not a desirable side effect of badass boots, it does illustrate that should you desire to swirl an element of contrariness, sass, or aplomb into your mix, boots with authority might be one way to do it. Additionally, you might want to do this spell if you're ready for your boots to "walk all over" someone in particular, perhaps someone who seemingly has been keeping you down (as in the Nancy Sinatra song, if you didn't already know what I was alluding to).

Find a pair of boots that lend themselves to a feeling of being a badass—in other words, buy them or fish them out of your closet. When the waxing moon is in Leo, Sagittarius, or Aries, place five Atomic Fire Balls (a kind of candy—substitute another form of wrapped cinnamon candy if these are unavailable) in each boot. Light ten sticks of cinnamon incense and hold them together as you bathe the boots in the smoke (hold a dish or incense holder beneath them to catch any burning embers).

Extinguish the incense. Leave the candy in the boots overnight, and then discard it. Wear the boots whenever you want to be sassy, confident, daring, or independent—or, you know, bitchy (in a good way).

General Shoe Magic

A number of magical rituals involve charming your shoes by placing magical items inside them overnight or until you next wear them. For example, a couple of gold coins, one in each shoe, will help you attract abundance. A pinch of mugwort in each shoe can help smooth your travel experience. Filling your shoes with fresh rosemary or mint will generally refresh your energy and help attract blessings and luck.

Scarves:
The Emanation of You

As Indian women and French women often demonstrate—in different and yet equally stunning ways—scarves can be employed to embellish and extend your attractiveness and personal energy. Like the glowing tail of a shooting star, a scarf can add movement and eye-catching flair when properly worn. Additionally, scarves are very versatile and can be used for a number of magical and sartorial purposes.

Speak Up and Be Heard: Scarf Spell I

When balanced and activated, the throat chakra—the energy center located at your neck/throat area—enhances clear, balanced, effective, harmonious communication. This scarf spell can help for times when this is of the essence; for example, when you're speaking in public or when you are desperately in need of having a heart-to-heart talk with someone. It can also be helpful when you're generally working on balancing your throat chakra and communication.

Find a vibrant blue scarf that you love. It can be anywhere between the ranges of aqua or robin's-egg blue and jewel-toned cobalt or royal blue (but draw the lines at powder blue and navy). Cleanse a carnelian stone in bright sunlight or sage smoke for at least one or two minutes. Fold up the scarf and place the carnelian on top. Nearby, place a blue votive candle in a tall jar, then light it. Leave this overnight or until the candle burns all the way down, making sure the candle will be totally safe from animal friends, children, wind, etc. The next day, wear your scarf—and speak up and be heard!

Swaddled in Self-Love: Scarf Spell II

Beginning about a year ago, circumstances unfolded in such a way as to prompt me to do some more inner exploration and self-healing regarding the childhood abuse I experienced. One of the important discoveries I made was that I often escaped my physical body by neglecting to be conscious of its basic needs and the ways it was feeling. As you can imagine, this translated into feelings of emotional discomfort and general loneliness.

While I was working with this realization, I came upon a super soft, gauzy, light baby pink cotton scarf printed with feathers. My inner little girl loved it, and it had a swaddling, baby blanket quality to it when I felt it against my skin. Plus it was only seven dollars, so I bought it. I then wore it frequently as a symbol of self-care: I tied it around my waist if I was wearing a skirt, wrapped it around my shoulders as a shawl, or draped it around my neck. It served to remind me to take care of myself and to come into a loving awareness of my physical body. You might want to try something like this if you haven't been babying yourself enough or if you could use an extra dose of self-love.

Remember Me: Scarf Spell III

Perhaps you're going on a first date or you'd generally like to make a lasting impression on whomever you're spending time with. If so, try very lightly spritzing or anointing a flowy, attractive scarf with a scent that feels right (see the "Scent" section of the next chapter for guidance). Then hold it up to the light of the moon or hold it to your heart. Take a few deep breaths, relax, and focus your mind. While you're still holding it in both hands, say or think:

> **When I leave I still remain**
> **Like the scent after the rain**
> **In your thoughts I'll dance and sway**
> **At least one week after the day.**

Wear it as desired.

Flow Through the Day: Scarf Spell IV

I once read in a psychology book that even seemingly inconsequential day-to-day hassles add up to be a big contributor to our overall stress level. Since everything is energy, we can minimize this effect by getting into a more harmonious energetic flow—then not only will hassles begin to seem less stressful, but we will attract fewer hassles to begin with.

This ritual draws upon the flowy nature of scarves to help us flow through the day.

Find a flowy scarf that gives you a harmonious feeling— perhaps something reminiscent of a vacation or something in a color that you find especially soothing. Then, on a Saturday or a Wednesday when the moon is in Cancer, Pisces, or Libra, take it to a moving body of water or a lovely outdoor water feature such as a waterfall, a cascading yard or park fountain, the ocean, or a river. Hold it near or above the flowing water, and imagine the ions and flowing energy entering the scarf. Feel the feeling of harmony and flow, and imagine yourself smiling and sailing easily throughout your day. Wear whenever you're craving more harmony and flow.

Hats:
Whom Do You Want to Be Today?

As evidenced by the phrase "I wear many hats" and similar phrases such as "Time to put on my such-and-such hat," hats are symbolically synonymous with the roles we play in life. And as a hat enthusiast from way back (I was told that one of my high-school monikers was "the girl with the funky hats"), I feel that hats, perhaps more than any other clothing object, can put a very particular spin on your day and your feeling about yourself. In other words, if you want to give your day—or your image—a kick, it just might be the day to wear that hat (you know the one).

Confident Hat

If you'd like to have a simple little charm you can place on your head that will give you an immediate confidence infusion, take your time and find the right hat. Then place it in bright sunlight for a minute or two as you burn nine sticks of cinnamon incense and bathe it in the smoke. Extinguish the incense (then safely store for future use), hold the hat to your heart, close your eyes, and conjure up all the confidence that you possibly can. See yourself wearing that hat and going around expressing your confidence in the world. For example, you might see yourself starting mutually enjoyed conversations with strangers, speaking or dancing in public, or just wearing a self-confident little smile in the supermarket. Direct the energy of these thoughts and feelings into the hat, and wear as needed.

Incognito Hat

You know those paparazzi pictures in which the movie star is wearing a baseball cap and sunglasses? Obviously their incognito get-up may not have worked as well as they had hoped if they were captured in those pictures, but for every picture like that you see, there are probably plenty of times that it *did* work. It's sort of like an "in public but off-duty" sort of look, and it's still somehow glamorous. That is the kind of incognito hat I'm talking about. Mine is a black baseball cap that says VENICE in white letters. People notice it when I wear it, but I feel like they don't notice *me* exactly, at least not my innermost self. Plus I don't have to do my hair.

So, find your incognito hat. Then place an iron pyrite crystal in it (first cleanse it in sunlight or sage smoke). Leave the crystal in it while you store it to keep its under-the-radar power charged and refreshed.

Vests:
Protection, Abundance, or Authority

Granted, all vests are not bulletproof. Still, because they often cover your core and your most vital organs, they do feel quite protective. What's more, as they are associated with authorities on various subjects such as college professors or people who for whatever reason need to wear tuxedos or other fancy suits, and since you don't usually precisely need a vest but might wear them for fashionable purposes, you might say that they are associated with authority and affluence.

Bulletproof: *Vest of Protection*

If your magical goal is to protect yourself physically, energetically, or emotionally, in addition to taking every precaution possible and practical in the physical realm, you might want to empower a vest to protect you. This would also be a good idea if you're working through deep-seated fears regarding a particular situation and you'd like a magical boost.

Choose a vest that feels protective but also that merges seamlessly with whatever outfit you're wearing and whatever situation you're wearing it in. When the moon is full, light nine sticks of frankincense incense and bathe the vest in the smoke. Extinguish all but one of the sticks and place it in an incense holder. While it's burning, discreetly sew a small clove of garlic, along with a tiny white quartz crystal that has been cleansed in sunlight or white sage smoke, into a small pouch made from red cotton fabric. Safety-pin it to the inside of the vest. Call on Archangel Michael to imbue the vest with protective energy that will surround you whenever you wear it, then thank him. For example, you might simply say:

Archangel Michael, I call on you!

Please infuse this vest with your blindingly bright, fiery, protective light.

Whenever I wear it, may I be completely safe, surrounded, and shielded in all ways.

Thank you, thank you, thank you.

Blessed be. And so it is.

To refresh the magic, anoint the pouch with a bit of frankincense essential oil as desired.

Investment: Vest of Abundance

A vest might be a good clothing object to enchant for abundance purposes, such as during a job hunt, a gambling expedition, or a trip to the bank to apply for a loan. To create a vest of abundance, on a Thursday while the moon is waxing, lay a square of red or burgundy velvet out on a bed or table. Place the vest on it. Add nine allspice cloves, a citrine quartz crystal, and twelve one-dollar bills. Anoint with a wealth-drawing oil such as patchouli, cinnamon, or orange.

Fold it up in the vest and leave it until the full moon. To keep the magic fresh, continue to store the vest in the velvet or repeat the ritual.

Vested: Vest of Authority

For many years I taught gymnastics to children. During that time I learned that possessing authority is a knack. You have to develop the knack and then consciously wield it if you're going to run a safe and harmonious class. Indeed, a similar knack is required anytime you're called upon to exercise authority. If you're learning how to gracefully move into possession of that particular brand of power, you might want to magically employ a vest to help you make that step.

Choose a vest that you like and that feels like a good choice for your day, and also be sure that it's one your imagination recognizes as authoritative.

On a new moon while the moon is in Leo, Taurus, or Aries, spread the vest out on a table top or bed. Light a stick of frankincense and place it in a holder near the vest. Also place a white candle nearby. With a ritual knife or sword (or something that works for the occasion, such as a beloved pocketknife, a wand made from a tree branch, or a crystal wand that has been cleansed in sunlight or sage smoke), lightly touch each shoulder of the vest as if you are knighting it. Say:

> **I am now invested with exactly the
> wisdom and power I need.**
>
> **I step into my divinely designed role as
> authority figure, and I know just what to do.**

I teach what I need to teach, learn what I need
to learn, attract abiding respect from others,
and show respect where respect is due.

I gracefully accept my position, and I
embody it to the best of my ability.

Belts:
Protection and Strength

According to fashion expert Tim Gunn, "The belt can work magic, and it was considered literally magical in ancient times." He even suspects that an amulet on a belt may have been the very first article of clothing ever worn by humans—for protective magical purposes!

Additionally, in present-day culture, belts are often prizes in contests related to strength and physical power, such as in wrestling and weightlifting.

Safety Belt: Magical Protection

Since belts are circled around our midsection, they naturally promote protection, especially when donned with that objective. Additionally, a jeweled or shiny belt buckle or a buckle that otherwise feels symbolically protective (see the "Symbols" section in the next chapter) can accentuate this protective power and serve as a focal point for your intention.

Choose a belt that feels protective to you, bathe it in white sage smoke, and anoint it with essential oil of frankincense. Call on Archangel Michael to bless it with his protective light. As you wear it, visualize/imagine/feel it shielding you from all negativity and negative intentions.

Title Belt: Magical Strength and Authority

If you'd like to feel like you're the reigning champion of your own life, giving yourself a title belt might be a good way to remind yourself of this intention and to fortify your belief in yourself. Find a belt that feels right. Perhaps it's especially substantial or jeweled. Then, on the full moon, visualize it filled with and surrounded by very bright, sparkly white light. Hold it up over your head as if you have just won it, and say:

Victory! Victory! Victory!

I am the reigning champion!

I walk with confidence and bravely
shine my light in the world!

Put it on and do a victory dance. Then wear it as desired.

Striped Tights:
The Witchiest of Accessories

Ever wonder why witches and fairies are so often depicted wearing striped tights? I can't tell you for certain, but I can tell you how I personally came to wear them, which may shed some light on the phenomenon in general. Not long after my first book, *Magical Housekeeping*, was released, I found myself invited to a pretty big Pagan convention to do a presentation. I was very intimidated. When I was still at home deciding what to pack, something told me to walk down to the ocean-front walk near where I live to see if I could find some multicolored striped tights. Lo and behold, the first shop I perused had precisely the ones that had flashed into my mind's eye. The first day I was at the conference, I felt very intimidated and pretty positive that I didn't belong. Two days later when I did my presentation, however, I wore the tights, and something magical happened. Not only did I suddenly feel right at home, but my presentation was packed! It went over very well, and my book was suddenly in high demand. On the outside, it might look like there were a number of reasons for my positive experience, but I happen to know it was the tights (who were known henceforth as my magic tights). I can only imagine that witches through the ages have had similar experiences, perhaps explaining why striped leggings have been so popular with witchy folk over the years.

Maybe your magic tights will call to you someday—or maybe they are calling to you right now! If so, be sure to follow the call.

The Three Secrets

In traditional Tibetan feng shui there is something known as the Three Secrets Empowerment. But it is not only Tibetan; when it comes to magical and mystical practices, it appears across the board. Essentially, the three secrets boil down to:

1. Gesture
2. Vocalization
3. Visualization

Of course, all of these are chosen, executed, and woven together by a specific intention.

To illustrate what I'm talking about, think of a yogi doing a yoga pose while chanting a chant and expecting a particular brand of well-being. Or think of a magician with a long white beard flicking his wand and saying a magic word while creating a clear mental picture of what is desired. When I was a little girl, my dad used to read us a book called *Strega Nona* in which the main character, whose name translated from Italian to "Grandma Witch," made pasta in her magical pasta pot by saying magic words, expecting pasta, and then blowing three kisses. Again, the three secrets!

The reason I bring these up is that you can create your own Three Secrets Empowerment to empower your clothes and accessories with magical energy. Here's how.

First, choose your intention, and write it down as if it is already true. Make sure it has to do with your positive beliefs about yourself, as this is what will magnetize your desire in the most ideal and effective way. Don't choose an intention that has to do with changing other people, especially any specific person. In other words, it won't ultimately benefit you to choose an intention like "Mike falls in love with me" or "Everyone gives me what I want." Instead, your intention might be something like:

- I am wealthy.

- I exude confidence.

- I sparkle with beauty.

- I easily manifest all the desires of my heart.

- I love everyone and everyone loves me. (Even though this does incorporate other people into the intention, it starts with you and has to do more with the energetic exchange and the expectation of positivity than the intention to simply control other people.)

Once you've written this intention down, choose a gesture to go with it. Here are a few ideas, but don't feel limited by them. If your spiritual practice (yoga, meditation, magic, etc.) possesses other gestures that feel right to you, feel free to choose those.

Gestures

Prayer Pose: Bring your hands to your heart level with flat palms pressed together in classic prayer position.

- Ideal for intentions related to serenity, beauty, grounding, happiness, and general positivity.

- This pose smooths energy and grounds your intention in love.

Expelling Mudra: This is basically a flicking motion. Holding your palms toward the object you're empowering, curl your ring and middle fingers under your thumb, and then flick them outward with each vocalization (see below for vocalization suggestions).

- Ideal for intentions related to strength, power, purification, protection, and dynamic positivity.

- This pose activates energy, cleanses negativity, and creates a potent magical charge.

Jupiter Mudra: With fingers interlaced, extend index fingers in a pointing position toward object to be empowered.

- Ideal for intentions related to focus, success, overcoming obstacles, and dissolving barriers.

- This pose creates an expansive and magnetic energy field.

Vocalizations

Now choose a vocalization related to your intention. To keep it simple, you could simply use your intention (as written above) as your vocalization and choose to chant it three, six, or nine times. Three has a simplicity to it, six resonates with the planet Venus and the energy of love, and nine has the most potent and dynamic power. (If you're chanting something nine times, to keep track in your mind, you can think of chanting it three times and then repeat that three times.) To keep it even simpler, you could shorten your intention to its most essential word or phrase, such as "Success," "Love," or "Prosperity," and again choose to chant it three, six, or nine times.

Or you could choose a mantra that you like and that feels right for your purpose. For example, you might choose to chant:

- "Om" three times for peace and general positivity.

- "Aham Prema" ("I am Divine Love") six times to magnetize beauty, love, and romance.

- "Gobinday, Mukunday, Udaray, Aparay, Hariang, Kariang, Nearnamay, Akamay," ("Sustainer,

Liberator, Enlightener, Infinite, Destroyer, Creator, Nameless, Desireless") nine times to dissolve obstacles and open you up to prosperity, success, and all forms of blessings.

Another alternative would be to vocally call on a deity who helps with intentions such as yours, such as Lakshmi or Abundantia for wealth, Aphrodite for love, Diana or Isis for personal power, or Archangel Michael for protection. In this case, you could just say the deity's name, or you could say something like "Lakshmi, I call on you!" or "Archangel Michael, please lend your protection!"

Visualizations

Finally—or more precisely before, during, and after your gesture and vocalization—you will want to visualize the completion and manifestation of your desire. To do this, as if you are daydreaming, conjure up the visions and feelings associated with experiencing what you desire. As much as possible, get into the feeling that they are already present in your life experience. This is what will magnetize them to you.

If you feel intimidated by this, don't! It is actually quite easy, and it will get even easier the more you do it.

Presto Change-O

This section is for those of you who attribute a certain exclusive, highly desirable magic to high-priced designer items and yet don't always (or ever) feel comfortable spending as such. Being a magical fashionista, of course, you need suffer no longer. Let me explain.

I once read an article in a fashion magazine about some duchess or princess (someone royal, at any rate) who wore a suit from a certain discount megastore to a super highbrow society party as a social experiment. The result? Naturally, everyone assumed it was tailor-made for her by some internationally recognized designer.

Indeed, countless style experts assert that with ingenuity you can achieve designerlike looks even when the bulk of your wardrobe is from thrift stores, clothes swaps, and discount stores. To take this a step further, I believe that if you wear something with the same degree of confidence and pride that you would wear it if it were custom-made for you by, say, Valentino, it will appear indisputably stylish and chic. (Naturally, you have to genuinely like it and believe in it before you can do this with authenticity.)

Did you ever see that *I Love Lucy* episode in which Lucy goes on a hunger strike until Ricky agrees to get her a Paris gown? Instead, he makes her a crazy get-up made of burlap and tells her it's from a brand-new line that hasn't been released yet. After a designer sees her proudly wearing the fake couture, his newest line is an obvious ripoff of the ensemble. Clearly, it was her confidence that did the trick.

So, for example, perhaps you have a black dress in your closet that you got on clearance from the local boutique down the street. As you gaze at it on the hanger, at first you might think of the clearance rack: the red slash through the price tag, for example. Then, in order to begin to turn it into a designer dress with the power of your mind, you might begin to think of how excellent it looks on you. "It really does look tailor-made," you think. "You know, it looks just as good as those dresses in the Marc Jacobs fall collection. Come to think of it, I would rather have this dress than any one of those dresses. It's so much more versatile and unique. I'm so lucky I found it and that it fits me so perfectly. Thank goodness I know how to shop!" Then, when you put it on, look at yourself in the mirror and really imagine for a minute that it cost at least ten times more than it actually did. Imagine exactly how lovely you would feel in it if it did cost that much. Now ask yourself: what's the harm in feeling that lovely in it anyway? And seriously, why not?

Another way to do this would be to make it into a fun little game to play with yourself. Remember when you used to be a kid and pretend that a blanket was Wonder Woman's cape? (You do? Me too!) Or remember that acting class during which you put yourself in the headspace of a farm girl or a medieval queen? Same concept. You might think to yourself: *What if this skirt were a designer skirt? What if I did pay 500 dollars for it?* Then behave as if it were true.

Finding Your Fashion Angel

Let me remind you once again that this chapter is called "You Are a Magician." And when you think magician, do you think Prospero from *The Tempest*? I do. Remember how he had that pet angel, Ariel, to help him achieve his magical aims? Well, as a magical fashionista—and a magician—whether you realize it or not, you probably already have a fashion angel. For our purposes, I mean someone in the spiritual realm whom you sartorially idealize or from whom you draw inspiration. This could be a deceased loved one (perhaps a glamorous grandma who used to take you shopping), a deceased celebrity (Cleopatra or Cristóbal Balenciaga, maybe?), or a divine helper (such as Aphrodite or Archangel Jophiel, the angel of beauty). If a fashionable and/or beauty-related noncorporeal being doesn't spring to mind immediately, take a few moments to relax. Close your eyes and take some deep breaths, then set the intention to discover who that being is. You might say or think, "I now open myself to connecting with my fashion angel. My mind is open and alert to discovering his or her identity, and I do so easily and quickly." You might like to finish up with "Thank you, thank you, thank you. And so it is."

Once you know who your angel is, you can call on him or her before you go shopping and whenever you want a little extra help getting dressed. You might just take a quick moment to silently think something like, "Grandma, please help me to find the perfect handbag at a perfect price!" or "Cleopatra, I am grateful to you for guiding me to assemble the most mesmerizing outfit that is ideal for the occasion in every way. Thank you!" You might even consider creating a little altar to your fashion angel near your closet or on your dresser. Then you can light a candle or burn incense as an act of devotion and to help keep you aligned with his or her energy.

7

you are
A GURU

To some, opening the closet and deciding what to wear is an exercise in monotony. To others, it's a vehicle of frustration and self-abuse. But now, to you, it is a sacred act. It is an opportunity to celebrate the day, to adorn and express your own divinity, and to align your inner vision with your outer reality. As you continue to live this way, the more you see firsthand and know beyond a shadow of a doubt that your clothing choices and self-care practices can be—when treated as such—nothing short of magical.

One of these days, you're going to have to admit it: in an uncommonly mystical sense, you are your own fashion guru. The contents of this chapter are all about helping you add even more dimension and depth to your spiritually sartorial powers.

> Fashion is
> part of the daily
> air and it changes
> all the time, with all the
> events. You can even see the
> approaching of a revolution in clothes.
> You can see and feel *everything* in clothes.
> DIANA VREELAND, ICONIC EDITOR AND CURATOR

Deciding What to Wear

So far, we've covered a lot of ways to zero in on what you feel good in and what will enhance your intentions and mojo on any given day. Now let's talk about the actual act of choosing what to wear.

First of all, as we talked about earlier, you might like to make a note of the day of the week and the sign that the moon is in just to get an idea of the prevailing energies—and corresponding color groups—of the day. Then consider the things you're expecting to experience. What are you doing today? Where will you be? Who will you be with? How do you want to feel? You might close your eyes and imagine yourself in this situation (work, a concert, yoga class, the grocery store, or whatever it is). Or, if you don't

know what's in store, that's great too! Embrace the possibilities and consider what positive feelings you'd like to feel,
regardless of what you're doing or who you may encounter.
Instead of just thinking of how you'd like to feel, *feel* how
you'd like to feel today. Then ask yourself: *When I feel this
way, what am I wearing? What feels just right?*

Imagine that the day is a swiftly flowing river of energy.
What you're doing when you get dressed in this way, energetically speaking, is like aligning yourself and your desires
with this river of energy in a way that will allow you to sail
smoothly and harmoniously in the direction of your dreami-
est and most divinely successful life experience.

So, to continue walking you through this sacred act of
getting dressed, you might notice that it's a Wednesday
and the moon is in Libra. At this time, yellow, lavender, and
gray things in your wardrobe might particularly catch your
eye. Then, you might think to yourself: *As I vacuum the floors,
answer my emails, buy produce at the farmers' market, and then go
out to dinner with my family today, I want to feel flowy and special. I want to feel like everything I do is a sacred act, and like my
heart is open and full of love.* You close your eyes and feel these
feelings as you imagine yourself doing the things you have
planned. Then, when you open your eyes, you have nar-
rowed down your wardrobe even more: skinny jeans, gauzy
white tank, lacy buttercream shawl, owl charm necklace,
beaded flip-flops. You try them on.

Maybe they're perfect or maybe you continue fine-tuning.
Hmmm, no, maybe a bit more casual, you think, and try on the
cutoff shorts instead. *Or perhaps a little more feminine,* so you

try on a long hippie skirt or tie on a flowery scarf. This is all a part of the alchemical calibration of aligning how you want to feel and what you'd like to experience with how you look.

Remember that every day—no matter how casual your plans—is special! Looking your best will help you feel your best. So take your time, be mindful, and wait until you get that inner yes. (It might also be helpful to remember, as I do, Tim Gunn's admonishment: "If you wouldn't want to run into an ex-lover, that's a sure sign you could do better.")

The rest of the information in this chapter will help you choose your outfits with mastery of both practical and mystical varieties.

Proportion

Remember when we looked in the mirror? Let's do that again. Look at your facial features. Compared to the rest of

It is essential that I dress based on my mood in order to feel more confident. A certain outfit can make me feel like a million bucks one day, and on another day it can bear absolutely no oomph.

ERIN JANE AMABILE,
MAGICAL FASHIONISTA

your body, do they appear small, medium, or large? Also, are they compact (close together), spread apart, or moderately spaced? Do you have a round, long, or heart-shaped face that appears larger in comparison to the rest of your body, or do you have a more diminutive face in comparison to the rest of your body?

If your face, head, and features appear small compared to the rest of your body (regardless of the actual size of either) or if your features are compact, smaller and more delicate prints and accessories will be most likely to become you.

If your face, head, and features appear large compared to the rest of your body (regardless of the actual size of either) or if your features are generously spaced, larger and more prominent prints and accessories will be most likely to become you.

And, naturally, if you feel that the proportional relationship between your face, head, features, and body are average, average-sized prints and accessories will be most likely to become you.

This is not a hard and fast rule but rather a general framework that will help you choose clothes and accessories and recognize precisely why an item may be more or less likely to look great on you.

Here's one more proportion-related tip that I find to be especially helpful: notice the distance between the bottom of your chin and the top of your forehead (at your hairline). Now, using this measurement, notice the spot on your chest that is an equal distance downward from the bottom of your chin. This is an important point: when you emphasize it in some way (via neckline placement, a pendant, or the knot in a scarf), it will usually appear balanced and will highlight your features and appearance in a beautiful, artful way. To give you an idea of how I make use of this tip, when I have a neckline that falls above or below this point, I will find a necklace with a pendant that falls to it. When I shop for garments, knowing about this point helps me find pieces with necklines that are most uniquely suited to me. This tip also comes in handy when choosing necklaces, buttoning shirts, and deciding how to wear a scarf.

Shapes

Similarly, it can help to look at the shapes that appear in your facial features. For example, my eyebrows arch up to a point, and the middle top area of my lips appears as two little points. This subtle motif in my face (which is also an aspect of my fiery elemental makeup—see chapter 3) makes it so that prints, garments, and accessories with V-necks and angles, such as stars, diamonds, triangles, and zigzags, are more likely to enhance my appearance.

So look at the shapes of your eyes, eyebrows, nose, lips, chin, cheekbones, hairline, and entire face. What shapes and lines do you see? Almond eyes, a heart-shaped mouth, arched eyebrows, round cheeks, or a square-shaped face? Choosing prints and accessories with shapes that in some way mirror these shapes will be more likely to shine a spotlight on your radiant beauty.

Symbols

Gurus and shamans of all ages—even modern ones such as psychologists and ad executives—have recognized the vast power of symbols to affect our consciousness and color our experience of life. So, when choosing clothing and accessories, it can be helpful to be aware of the meaning and power of the symbols they depict. Below, you'll find a guide to some popular prints and accessory symbols. If you're curious about the symbolism of something that isn't listed here, or if you're looking for a symbol to represent a particular energy in order to fuel a particular intention, you might want to do an Internet search or check out a symbol dictionary such as *The Element Encyclopedia of Secret Signs and Symbols* by Adele Nozedar.

Animal prints of any kind are very fiery and fun. They add a sense of warmth, wildness, and freedom.

Ankhs are symbols of rebirth.

Argyle is a more dynamic, fiery version of earthy plaid. It energizes and accentuates social pursuits while also emphasizing family and interconnection.

Birds have long been considered to be divine messengers and intermediaries between the earthly and heavenly realms. They also represent the air element, which includes thought, words, and imagination.

Butterflies represent positive transformation, domestic or marital bliss, and freedom.

Circles, ovals, and polka dots bring in energies related to the heavenly realm, creativity, synchronicity, birth, seeds, fertility, and focus.

Clovers represent the threefold Celtic goddess, the Holy Trinity, luck, and health.

Diagonal stripes have a dynamism and movement that evokes the fire element, which enhances energy, radiance, and bright vivaciousness.

Diamond and triangle shapes have a dynamic, energized, fiery quality.

Fleur de lis symbols and patterns represent the Mother Goddess, as well as royalty and refinement. They can help align us with our natural, divinely bestowed right to experience all forms of blessings and abundance.

Flowers and floral prints represent romance, femininity, optimism, and personal growth.

Horizontal stripes, like the horizon for which they are named, are evocative of the earth element and therefore promote coziness, tradition, and groundedness.

Horses represent freedom, independence, wildness, and personal power.

Lotus flowers represent peace, wisdom, and spirituality.

Moon and crescent shapes represent the Goddess (or the divine feminine), receptivity, femininity, intuition, cycles, and spirituality.

Owls, in addition to the qualities listed in the "birds" section, represent wisdom, intuition, and the ability to see into the truth of a matter.

Paisley has a creative, free, flowy quality. Paisley prints enhance artistic endeavors and dreamy flights of the imagination.

Pentacles represent the dynamic, active, magical quality within elemental balance and the entire natural world.

Plaid has a very earthy, grounded energy, and also represents strength, family, and interconnection.

Spirals are the symbol that countless ancient cultures used to represent the cosmos long before our species had scientifically documented that our galaxy was spiral shaped. Spiral symbols represent pure divine creativity, cosmic consciousness, expansive awareness, pure potentiality, and interconnection with All That Is. A spiral can also symbolize womb energy (or divine feminine creativity).

Squares and rectangles resonate with the energy of solid foundations and the earth.

Star and sun shapes are bright, warm, sparkly, radiant, and generally reminiscent of the fire element. Sun shapes can also represent the divine masculine principle.

Tie dye has a lot to do with the color and pattern but always possesses a watery, dreamy, creative quality. When it contains reds and other bright warm colors, it can also be very fiery and flamelike, especially when it depicts a radial shape.

Vertical stripes, like a forest of trees, bring in the wood element and therefore facilitate growth, energy, and upward movement.

Wavy lines possess the flowy, dreamy, fluid energy of the water element.

Zigzags and lightning bolts are fiery and dynamic. They feel powerful, bright, energetic, and fun.

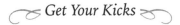

Get Your Kicks

My friend Courtney once got on a black turtleneck and jeans kick for almost an entire season. Sometimes I'll go weeks when I want to wear girly hippie skirts and jewelry and then switch into a period during which a comfy T-shirt and jeans feel like the most harmonious and nourishing choice. We all go through phases and get on kicks, and it's important to be awake to what feels right in the moment and then go with it.

Colors

Colors are literally vibration: the optical experience of each is dictated by the frequency at which it vibrates. Although we've already discussed colors from the angle of the elements, our own embodiment of a particular natural setting, and the astrological influences of the day, it can be helpful to be aware of the psychological and metaphysical properties of colors and color groups when choosing outfits for particular intentions.

Please keep in mind that everyone possesses his or her own unique energy and vibratory properties, so each color will blend with your energy in its own unique way. For this reason, it can be helpful to tune in to your intuition to learn how you personally relate to each color. For instance, you might like the look of burgundy in your living room décor, but how do you feel when you wear it, and how do you look? As another example, you might already know that you love pink, and, upon closer investigation, you may discover that dustier pinks become you more than brighter ones.

Bright red is pure fire, and it facilitates fame, energy, radiance, courage, success, and expansion. It can be helpful for performances and anytime you'd like to stand out from the crowd.

Brick red is fire mixed with a dose of earth. It's a bit more grounded, though it still promotes expansion and radiance. It can be especially fortifying for endeavors that require bravery and confidence.

Terra cotta is exceptionally grounding, though still fiery and expansive. With its warm earthiness, it is a red tone that is especially suited to supporting interpersonal relationships, and it can therefore be a good choice for peacemaking endeavors and social pursuits.

Burgundy mixes the earth element with a deep, smoldering fire energy. It's a red that blends its native fire element with the energies of luxury, elegance, and wealth.

Pale pink is exceptionally feminine, and it brings stillness, clarity, and serenity to the mind while simultaneously enhancing the soft, gentle, loving qualities of the heart and emotions.

Bubblegum pink is relaxing and heart opening. It exudes and enhances youthfulness, romance, and charm.

Hot pink is a more feminine and less aggressive version of bright red: just as fiery, it leans its fire energy more toward sexuality and playfulness than confidence and career success.

Fuchsia, a deep pink that leans toward purple, takes the playful energy of hot pink a bit deeper, as it broaches the realm of elegance, magic, and creative inspiration.

Bright orange does not become a huge number of us fashion-wise. Unfortunately, in our culture it is evocative of prison and utility garments. Still, for those of us who can wear it well (and want to), it can be a fiery, expansive color with strong elements of grounding and earth.

Burnt orange is earthy, grounding, and warming to the heart and emotions. Like a sunset or a pumpkin, it emits a vibration of satisfaction and coziness.

Peach is warming, soothing, heart opening, and romance enhancing. Like the fruit for which it is named, it is fuzzy and sweet.

Bright yellow, like bright orange, is not for everyone. Still, for those of us who can wear it, it's exceptionally earthy and lends itself to a clear, focused mind.

Pale yellow or buttercream is grounding, calming, and relaxing. Mostly the metal element with a strong streak of earth, it facilitates clear thinking and is helpful for any time when details and precision are of the essence.

Goldenrod is an elegant way to wear yellow. Like saffron, it exudes luxury and evokes earthy delights. Tibetan monks employ it in the color of their robes, perhaps because it also promotes serenity and presence of mind.

Kelly green or grass green, the color of clovers and healthy grass, is pure prosperity and health. Also aligned with the heart chakra and the ecological movement, it promotes loving connections between all living things.

Mint green, like mint itself, is fresh, enlivening, and energizing. It brings clarity to the mind and senses while vibrating at the frequencies of health, wealth, self-improvement, and harmonious communication.

Forest green is a grounded green that enhances a feeling of community and connection with other people and the planet. Like all greens, it is also supportive of health, wealth, and prosperity.

Olive or army green is often employed to help one blend into one's surroundings undetected. Similarly, it can help us to feel at one with the ground and growing things. It is the most grounded and earthy of all greens.

Teal is aligned with the thymus and the immune system; as such, it can enhance health. And, as a combination of blue and green, it's very much in alignment with wealth and a healthy financial flow.

Turquoise facilitates healthy communication, creativity, inspiration, and joy. It's also a wealth and prosperity color.

Royal blue, cobalt blue, and electric blue are protective and magically transformative. They are aligned with the place where our emotions—painful or pleasant—transform themselves into harmonious and joyful flow. It feels markedly nourishing to wear these shades during times when these concerns are of the essence. They also feel good to wear when you'd like to protect yourself from negative energy and emotions (coming from yourself, others, or your environment).

Robin's-egg blue is soothing, uplifting, and energizing. Like turquoise, it promotes inspiration, joy, and healthy communication.

Pale or light blue helps bring more focus to the conscious mind and less focus to the senses and emotions. It can be helpful for times when one may benefit from temporarily pushing emotions and senses to the side, such as studying, taking your cat to the vet, or negotiating a financial deal.

Periwinkle blue, a medium blue with a healthy dose of lilac, is an exceptionally magical and romantic hue. It lends itself to intuition, inspiration, and a mystical worldview.

Navy blue is aligned with the deepest depths of the ocean, as well as emotional depth. It is nourishing to career success and successfully pursuing the truest and most authentic dreams of one's heart. Possessing both poetry and authority, it can be helpful for anytime you'd like to be taken seriously and anytime you'd like your creative input to be heard and respected.

Indigo is aligned with intuition and magic. It's also a very transformational color that helps to fine-tune one's energy and the energy in one's environment by transmuting negativity into positivity in the most ideal and harmonious of ways. It can be a good choice for times when you're traversing challenging energetic or emotional situations.

Violet or royal purple is aligned with the crown chakra and our connection with the Divine and the heavenly realm. It is another transformational color that can help us to be awake to the magic of life and to see the divine spark in everything. This is a good color to wear when you'd like to transcend "same old, same old" thinking and see everything through a more mystical lens. Additionally, because it is connected with the Divine and the realm of all possibility, it is a color of wealth and luxury.

Lavender or lilac is a combination of fire, water, wood, and metal: it's a highly dynamic blend of all the Chinese elements except for earth. As such, it can be employed to help one transcend overattachment to the earthly plane. Additionally, it can help infuse our earthly appearance and presence with an otherworldly beauty and charm. Like violet or royal purple, it is also aligned with the crown chakra and the realm of the Divine.

Plum is a very fortifying and heart-opening version of purple. It lends physical strength and facilitates peace and interpersonal relationships. It is also a prosperity color.

Eggplant is the earthiest purple. It can help ground your energy and focus your mind while enhancing wealth, prosperity, and luxury. For some, it can also be highly nourishing to the body and the immune system.

Black is the most extreme version of depth and can help us align with our truth and our most ideal career path. As a pure representation of the water element, it's also highly aligned with artistic, poetic, and philosophical pursuits.

Light gray, like marble or granite, is a potent representation of the metal element. It lends itself to precision, accuracy, focus, details, intelligence, and mathematical prowess.

Charcoal gray is the water element tempered with the metal element, and it is therefore aligned with one's deep authenticity and artistic flow, with an underlying structure of clear thinking and precision. Consider wearing it when both are of the essence.

White, as a pure representation of the metal element, possesses all the same qualities as light gray. However, because it is also the reflection of all colors of the rainbow, it is also highly aligned with the Divine, pure positivity, healing, transmutation, energetic calibration, and purification. It can be healing to wear it during prolonged periods of mourning, emotional turmoil, or anytime you'd like an extra dose of purity and divine intervention.

Cream is also a metal element representative, so it possesses the qualities of light gray but with a slightly warmer and more grounding, heart-opening quality.

Silver, along with all metallic colors, is technically a representative of the metal element. But when it shows up in clothing and accessories, it is often more aligned with receptive lunar energy (and therefore serenity, femininity, and healing). And if it noticeably sparkles or shines, it's also aligned with the fire element (and therefore expansion and radiance).

Gold also may technically be a metal, but in clothing and accessories gold is more aligned with solar energy (and therefore expansion, health, and brightness), as well as both the fire and earth elements. These factors, as well as its obvious association with the common symbolism of the precious metal, make it highly aligned with the energies of wealth and prosperity.

Brown is pure earth energy. It can be very grounding, soothing, and harmonizing.

Light brown or beige is earth combined with metal, and it is therefore very helpful for mental pursuits that concern the physical realm, such as earth sciences and mechanics. Conversely, physical pursuits that require exceptional focus and accuracy—such as archery, aviation, and acrobatics—can also benefit from these colors.

Chocolate brown lends itself to both earthiness and artistic pursuits, because the deeper the brown, the more nourished it is by the watery realm of depth, poetry, and flow. As proof, consider chocolate itself, which is both sensual (earthy) and authentically joyful (watery).

Your Power Palette

Everyone's energy signature is unique, so everyone interacts with and reacts to colors differently. With this in mind, you might like to use the color descriptions in this chapter as jumping-off points to discover your own unique, mystical color palette. To illustrate: working with the colors that look good on you, dusty pink may be your peace color and cerulean blue your wealth color. Shimmery gold might help you feel divinely magnetic; silver, divinely feminine. Take your time to determine a number of colors and their mystical or metaphysical meanings as they specifically pertain to you, and then consciously, pointedly, integrate these associations, perhaps by finding candles in each color, and then lighting them one at a time as you meditate on each respective quality. Continue to do this over a matter of months or even on an ongoing basis. You might also like to create a key to your palette and post it in the inside of your closet. (You might even employ a paint chip selection from the hardware store!) With the help of one or both of these practices, the power of the color will become even stronger for you, so that you can incorporate it in your wardrobe with an even greater degree of success.

Materials

Similarly, materials each lend their own unique energetic flavor to the mix. Here are some guidelines to the energetic properties of some popular materials.

> When I want to feel and communicate confidence, I typically wear vibrant oranges or grounding chocolate browns.
>
> RACHEL AVALON, HOLISTIC HEALTH COACH AND ECO-EXPERT

Please keep in mind that for the sake of kindness, I only recommend employing the faux (or, even though I never wear them myself, at least vintage, salvaged, or reclaimed versions of all animal-derived fabrics, including leather, wool, silk, feathers, cashmere, alpaca, camel hair, snakeskin, and so on). And I am hoping that soon we can all agree that real fur is never acceptable or attractive, even if it's reclaimed. It's like wearing your beloved pet—it sends the message that you are both heartless and tasteless.

Leather and faux leather—like all materials that appear to be (or are) animal-derived—lend themselves to a feeling of aliveness, warmth, and dynamism. These materials are also famous for their tendency to enhance one's rock-star quality.

Silk and silklike fabric has an elegant, steamy, water-meets-fire mystique. It's sensual and deepens one's capacity to both radiate and experience beauty.

Cotton has a nourishing, healthy, natural feeling. It's great for supporting endeavors related to spiritual, physical, and scholastic self-improvement.

Linen is elegant and comforting. It has the ability to infuse us with a crisp, clean, affluent feeling.

Woolens imbue us with a cozy, wholesome warmth. (Real wool, not so much.)

Flannel—famous for its role in plaid shirts and comfy pajamas—has a sensual, earthy softness that grounds us comfortably in our physical bodies.

Faux fur is playful, social, and fun.

Crochet, with its interwoven, handmade charm, reminds us of our roots: the earth, our family of origin, and our chosen family (a.k.a. friends). Additionally, its texture lends complexity, earthiness, and depth to the overall flavor of an outfit.

Lace can be feminine, sexy, delicate, or any combination of the three depending on its appearance and the way it's featured in an ensemble. It also lends texture and variety.

Denim has a fresh, simple, classic vibe. And, depending on how it's aspected, it can lend a sexy playfulness or a casual coziness to an ensemble.

Shimmery or sparkly materials can be either elegant (as in the case of a fitted sweater with hints of shimmery golden yarn woven through it) or fiery and fun (as in the case of a purse made of black material with shimmery silver sparkles).

Polarity

By virtue of being human, you possess a sexual essence. Regardless of your actual gender or your sexual orientation, it may lean more toward the masculine pole or the feminine pole. (In many cases, of course, females will have feminine essences and males will have masculine essences, but this is by no means true in every case.) Just like magnetic poles, neither is better or worse than the other: they are just different. And, when it comes to manifestation and creating the conditions we desire, polarity—or the magnetic dance between masculine and feminine sexual essences—is a very powerful force.

But before we begin to discuss the ways you might employ fashion to work with the power of your polarity, let's figure out the side of the polarity that you're naturally at home in. Generally speaking, feminine-essence people naturally desire to be admired and adored, crave love and connection, and revel in beauty and the senses. (Aromatic bubble bath? Yes, please!) And masculine-essence people prefer providing, protecting, accomplishing, and building their kingdom or empire. They also revel in the potential for adventure and escape. (Yes, this includes video games.)

Before you start to get concerned that I am perpetuating gender stereotypes, first remember that I am talking about your sexual essence, not your actual gender. Still, not long ago I also may have shied away from the idea that there are recognizably masculine and feminine traits. But then I read the books *Powerful and Feminine* by Rachael Jayne Groover and *Dear Lover* by David Deida, and my perspective changed. I began to realize that even though overcoming gender stereotypes is important for the sake of our cultural freedoms and expectations, for the sake of our personal healing and growth it *is* helpful to acknowledge that we have certain psychological and energetic attributes depending on our sexual essence. Learning about these and enhancing our polarity can help us feel more comfortable in our own skin, experience more harmony in our relationships, and magnetize the things we want. (As you may already know, and as I later learned, this way of thinking has been a part of tantric philosophies and modalities for centuries. When I excitedly told a couple of my esoterically inclined girlfriends about my polarity realizations, they were utterly unmoved and said something to the effect of, "Well, yeah. That's tantra.")

Because what we wear and how we treat ourselves has everything to do with the way we feel about ourselves and the messages that we silently send out into the world, fashion and self-care are excellent ways to amplify and celebrate our sexual polarity and personal magnetism.

If you have a feminine essence, the simple acts of lovingly attending to your wardrobe and self-care will enhance your polarity. You might also consider adding touches to your wardrobe that make you feel a bit more feminine. Never, of course, wear something that you don't like, but work within what you *do* like to find wardrobe enhancements that help you feel softer, curvier, prettier, more romantic, more nurturing, and more receptive (all feminine qualities). For example, perhaps you hate high heels, but maybe you could totally see yourself in a pair of ballet flats—and they absolutely put more of a feminine spring in your step than the old sneakers or penny loafers. Or maybe you've got to wear a suit for work, but you can definitely wear a sensual and beautifully colored undergarment or two, or choose accessories that sparkle or shine. Then again, maybe you want to get a little more openly girly: flouncy skirts, flowy scarves, high heels, lipstick, and the like. Or maybe letting your hair grow just a little bit longer or getting a new color will be just the thing. When it comes to enhancing your femininity and increasing your polar magnetism, follow your intuition and wear what feels right to you. Also remember to enjoy moving and being in your body.

It's important
for me to feel feminine
in some way…I feel more
comfortable showing a little bit
of curve with my silhouette. I tend
to wear a lot of jeans and T-shirts,
but I've found soft, semi-fitted tees
with feminine necklines that I like
and fitted jeans that aren't too
tight or uncomfortable.
EMILY WHITEHURST,
MUSICIAN

It's important to note, also, that another variation on magnifying polarity to enhance your femininity is with juxtaposition, by playing with masculine pieces such as tailored suits, short haircuts, and slacks in a masterful and intentional way. (If you want visuals, consider Diane Keaton in the movie *Annie Hall*, Isabella Rossellini's slicked-back hairdo, and any given lingerie model wearing a tie.)

Enhancing masculine polarity is the same concept, only reversed. If this is your intention, what feels masculine to you? Perhaps a solid color will feel more masculine than a print, or plaid will feel more masculine than paisley. Similarly, you might add more ruggedness to your haircut or facial hair situation, or more simplicity to the pattern of your suit. When it comes to the way you move and interact with the world, focused and destination-centered movements and actions will help you get into the most harmonious alignment with your polarity.

To play with reverse polarity to enhance your masculinity from a different angle, you might play with more traditionally feminine aspects, such as pink, longer hair, or sensual fabrics. (Think Keith Richards with his signature eyeliner, Russell Simmons during his pink period, or—for an exaggerated example of masculine energy emphasized by feminine aspects to the attire—a pirate.)

If the reverse-polarity thing seems contradictory at first, remember that it is simply a matter of playing with opposites. So, just as one may be equally likely to emphasize one's light brown eyes with light brown eye makeup (matching) or dark gray and black eye makeup (contrast-

I used to think that it was important to feel feminine all the time, but I have recently discovered the power of slightly more masculine apparel. Wearing things like blazers and tops that are a little less frilly without a lot of accessories makes me feel confident in a different way... It's like taking away the things that are obviously sexy (like short skirts and cleavage) makes me feel even sexier in a way.

ERIN JANE AMABILE,
MAGICAL FASHIONISTA

ing), you can work the polarity thing either way, as long as you are clear on which pole you are accentuating, and as long as you fully own and embody that polarity in your life and personality.

If you feel drawn to learn more about polarity, you might like to try studying tantra or reading the work of Rachael Jayne Groover or David Deida.

Scent

Our sense of smell is the sense most connected to our memories and emotions, so our scent, really and truly, has a highly potent and lasting psychological effect on the people we come into contact with. And, even more importantly, the scents we wear have a very potent effect on our *own* thoughts and emotions, which in turn affects every aspect of our life experience. (In fact, according to author and attractiveness expert Steven Dayan, MD, "Our personal scent is our calling card that introduces our background, health, and level of attractiveness to the world.") Indeed, two of the most iconic fashion icons of recent memory, Christian Dior and Coco Chanel, have both weighed in when it comes to the importance of perfume. Christian Dior has been quoted as saying, "A woman's fragrance says more about her than her handwriting," and Coco Chanel said, "A woman who doesn't wear perfume has no future." (I don't agree with the latter, of course, but I still get a kick out of it.)

Spraying or anointing ourselves with perfume is not the only way to smell good, however. If you have sensitive skin, or if you just like to maximize your options when it comes to scent, you might like to burn incense (safely!) in your closet or throw scented sachets or even small bags or boxes of incense into your clothing drawers. (There is an adorable import boutique in my neighborhood that always throws in a free little box of incense with your purchase—I furnish my drawers with them.)

As a matter of fact, we may not need actual perfume because so many things we use are already scented! Between laundry products, lotion, body washes or soaps, and hair products, we have the potential to have a lot going on in the fragrance department. And since a delicate—not overpowering or convoluted—scent is generally desirable, it might be a good idea to take inventory of all the scents you may already be emanating. Often, we habituate (or tune out) the scents that we smell on a regular basis or for a prolonged period, so you might not be able to smell all of them yourself, although this does not mean that other people can't smell them. In order to mitigate potential scent overwhelm—and to keep a clear palette in case you want to highlight a particular scent—you might want to choose fragrance-free options for all but one or two of the products that might add their own scent into the mix of your personal aroma.

All that being said, and keeping in mind that searching for natural and cruelty-free options is always best for us, animals, and the planet, the simplest and best way to choose a scent that will be powerful for you is to find one that you like and that gives you the type of feeling that you want to feel. You might try Whole Foods and other natural retailers. I like a brand called Pacifica that you can often find at Sephora. For more information about natural and cruelty-free options, check out peta.org.

Whether you choose a single note option (such as a safely diluted essential oil or basic perfume oil) or a fragrance blend, you might also like to keep in mind the metaphysical properties of various scents. For example:

Allspice draws love, luck, and wealth. It lends sweetness to the heart and coziness to one's experience of life.

Bergamot lifts the spirits, clears depression, and strengthens the aura. It's also energizing and alluring.

You Are a Guru

Cedar has a very grounding, sacred, spiritual vibe. It can help center and clear your mind while bringing you into your body and senses.

Cinnamon is warming, heart opening, and prosperity drawing.

Clove, like cinnamon, is warming and prosperity drawing. It's also soothing, grounding, and energizing.

Cocoa induces love and lust. It's also grounding and sensual, and it helps you feel like life is sweet.

Coconut brings a sense of sweetness, sustenance, luxury, and peace.

Copal is cleansing, protects from negativity, and attunes one to the subtle realm and the realm of spirits. It helps activate intuition and clear seeing.

Frankincense harmonizes the mind and clears the aura. It helps us to feel uplifted, grounded, and spiritually protected.

Gardenia supports health and beauty, and it infuses us with femininity, freshness, sweetness, and hope.

Geranium is highly balancing to the hormones and emotions. It's also exhilarating, stress reducing, and heart opening.

Ginger is both energizing and comforting. It brings clarity to the mind and warmth to the body and heart.

Grapefruit is energizing, cleansing, and uplifting. It facilitates exercise and helps us make healthy food choices.

Hyssop, according to authors Richard Alan Miller and Iona Miller in *The Magical and Ritual Use of Perfumes*, "assures faithfulness of friends and lovers, financial success, and protection during exorcism." It's also soothing to the emotions and uplifting to the mind.

Jasmine is an aphrodisiac. It's feminine, sensual, and sweet, and it has an enticing energetic depth.

Juniper is very cleansing, energizing, and soothing. It's also said to help regulate the appetite and to help with menstrual challenges.

Lavender is very calming and clarifying. It can both soothe and energize. It's also very healing on every level: mind, body, and spirit.

Lemon is super fresh, uplifting, energizing, and cleansing to the mind and senses.

Lilac is whimsical, soothing, and heart opening. It helps us to see beyond the veil and tune in to the realm of spirits.

Lime uplifts, focuses, and energizes the mind, and it helps heal depression.

Lotus blends well with other scents, lending dimension, depth, and harmonious synergy.

Myrrh lends a spiritual and meditative tone to fragrance blends while helping us ground our energy, find balance and harmony, and heal the mind, body, and spirit.

Narcissus is the scent of early springtime. It helps align us with fairy energy and with pure light and positivity. It also draws sweetness, beauty, and romance.

Neroli is soothing, heart opening, and sensual. It can be employed to help manifest a marriage or a desirable marriagelike relationship.

Nutmeg is an energizer, tonic, and aphrodisiac. It brings sweetness, warmth, and luck, and it protects from negativity.

Orange is warm, uplifting, soothing, and sweet. It can also help draw wealth and prosperity.

Palmarosa, a roselike scent, is very soothing, relaxing, healing, and heart opening.

Palo Santo is very grounding and cleansing. It protects from negativity (including negative entities and energy patterns), aligns us with divine energy, and helps us get into a positive life momentum.

Patchouli draws both passionate, sensual love and luxurious wealth. It's grounding and harmonizing. (On the other hand, I have been told that some people absolutely can't stand the scent of patchouli. Personally, I can't fathom this, but it bears paying attention to in case one of these people is someone with whom you regularly come into contact.)

Peppermint is refreshing, clarifying, and energizing. It awakens and focuses the mind and lifts the spirits. The scent also helps steady the stomach and soothe digestion.

Pine is energizing, cleansing, and healing. It's also fortifying to the health and emotions.

Plumeria is sweet, romantic, and harmonizing, and it has the free, joyful energy of an island vacation. It can also help with creative pursuits.

Rose is both very romantic and very spiritual. It can help increase self-love and magnetize beautiful, romantic conditions.

Rose geranium is very balancing and stabilizing for the emotions. It also supports physical and emotional health and opens the heart.

Rosewood relieves stress and helps energize the mind and body in a healthy, balanced way. It's also an aphrodisiac.

Sandalwood is both sensual and spiritual. It can help draw and facilitate inspiration, romance, and deep spiritual connection. It's also very grounding.

Spearmint is relaxing, soothing, and clarifying. It draws wealth and helps heal a broken or grief-stricken heart.

Sunflower, the fragrance of pure sunshine, is brightening, strengthening, sustaining, and expansive. It draws positivity and abundance.

Tangerine lifts the mood, soothes stress, and helps clear away fear and stagnation. It also draws wealth and luck. Tangerine helps us release mental chatter and come into the present moment.

Tuberose emanates pure desire, sensuality, deep relaxation, and endless mystique. Perfume with notes of tuberose can be like a passion potion, emphasizing attraction, physicality, and present-moment awareness rather than intellectualism and linear focus.

Vanilla is comforting, nurturing, and warm. It enhances and draws sweetness, coziness, and romance.

Vetiver is grounding and masculine. It can help increase one's energetic potency while magnetizing wealth and success.

Ylang ylang is highly sensual and stress relieving. It soothes the senses and helps get us out of our heads and into our bodies. This enhances romance, passion, creativity, femininity, and joy.

8

you are
ADOR(N)ABLE

This chapter is about accent and sparkle: jewelry and other accessories, makeup, and nail polish—you know, the extras. Not *always* necessary, but sometimes, you know, *totally* necessary.

Gemstones

Before we talk about the various types of jewelry, let's talk about gems and minerals: those lovely, magical little gifts from the earth that not only look so fetching as ornaments on our bodies but also possess metaphysical properties that can help us manifest our intentions and enhance our experience of life.

Generally speaking, if you're drawn to a certain mineral, there is a metaphysical reason for that. You might think of it as your intuition acting through your aesthetic sense to magnetize you to a certain crystalline energy that will bring

> We are meant
> to celebrate the good
> things of this earth. Pretty
> leaves, rocks, candles, sea
> treasures—all these remind
> us of our creator.
>
> JULIA CAMERON, AUTHOR
> AND CREATIVITY GURU

benefits to you at this particular time in your life. So a good rule of thumb is to notice which stones you're drawn to and then consider adorning yourself with them. You can check out their properties later and think, "Oh, no wonder I was drawn to that" or "Oh, how interesting, I guess I *have* been craving more clarity."

Still, you might also want to become familiar with their properties now, and then if you find there's one that sounds like something you could use, you could check it out in a store and see if you're also drawn to it aesthetically.

Here you'll find a sampling of the metaphysical properties of some common minerals used in jewelry, but if you'd like a more complete guide, there are plenty of books on the subject available. I'm personally a longtime devotee of *Love Is In The Earth* by Melody.

Agate is grounding, purifying, clarifying, wealth drawing, and ego eradicating. It also helps with articulation and self-expression.

Amethyst is restful, soothing, cleansing, and spiritual. It raises positive energy, enhances wisdom, and helps promote sobriety and curb addictive tendencies.

Aquamarine is purifying, mood lifting, and joy enhancing. It also helps clarify skin and detoxify the liver.

Carnelian is grounding, energizing, and strengthening. It enhances confidence, communication, and public speaking.

Citrine is wealth drawing, energizing, and mood lifting. It lifts depression, enhances optimism, and brings happiness and a sunny disposition.

Diamond symbolizes constancy and strength. Extremely fortifying, it aligns us with our deepest authenticity and beauty. Diamonds must be chosen and worn with integrity, both with regard to the physical selection of the diamond (no blood diamonds) and spiritual intentions (no gold digging), otherwise the energetic effects become undesirable.

Emerald is wealth drawing and vitalizing. It enhances health, love, and creativity.

Fluorite is purifying, clarifying, and energizing. It enhances organization and focus, and it clears and purifies skin.

Garnet is grounding, sensual, and passionate. It draws and enhances love and wealth.

Gold is strengthening, wealth enhancing, and heart opening. It is aligned with the energy of the sun.

Hematite is grounding, strengthening, energizing, and vitalizing. It enhances focus and will.

Herkimer diamonds enhance peace, intuition, clarity, harmony, and gentle alignment with divine energy and wisdom. (P.S.: They're not really diamonds.)

Jade is wealth drawing, spiritual, softening, soothing, and peace enhancing. Jade has very gentle, feminine energy that is believed to enhance luck.

Jasper is grounding, heart opening, and love drawing. It softens harsh energies, heals the body/mind/spirit, brings positivity, optimism, and joy.

Lapis lazuli heals the inner child, brings wealth and luck, and enhances creativity. It is energizing and uplifting.

Moonstone is a very receptive stone that absorbs negativity and enhances receptivity, intuition, femininity, and alignment with the moon. It must be cleansed often (see page 182).

Obsidian is very absorbent of harsh and negative energies; as such, it is very protective. Like moonstone, it must be cleansed often (see page 182).

Opal is the medium's stone and the stone of spirits. It enhances connection with the otherworld realm, so it's not recommended unless this sounds desirable to you (mediums and ghost enthusiasts, you know who you are).

Peridot is grounding and cleansing. It enhances health and vitality, soothes anxiety, promotes organization and cleanliness, and draws wealth.

Platinum is grounding, centering, aligning, and health enhancing. It benefits interpersonal relationships and promotes balance and harmony on all levels.

Rose quartz is healing, soothing, pain relieving, heart opening, and protective. It promotes healing sleep and positive dreams, dispels harshness and negativity, enhances health, and brings softness and harmony to relationships.

Ruby enhances love, romance, protection, happiness, and joy. It opens and harmonizes the heart and attracts wealth and positive beliefs and expectations with regard to finances.

Sapphire brings peace, balance, positivity, cleansing, and activating. It facilitates success in all life areas by bringing all things into focus and alignment.

Silver is harmonizing, soothing, and receptive, and is aligned with the moon.

Sodalite enhances logical thought and focus, allowing one to see the truth within situations. It supports harmony within groups, promotes authenticity, and soothes emotional imbalances.

Smoky quartz is cleansing, grounding, and focusing. It absorbs negativity, balances excess mental energy, and quiets mental chatter.

Topaz is bright, soothing, gentle, and mood-lifting. It promotes general positivity like gentle, warm sunshine.

Tourmaline brings confidence, protection, positivity, harmony, and balance.

Turquoise is good for protection, mental and emotional healing, strength, and drawing wealth. It promotes synchronicity and flow, and it is aligned with masculine energies and the heavenly realm.

White quartz is generally cleansing and energizing. It focuses and intensifies intentions, and helps us manifest our visions into form. It also brings clarity, aligns us with spirituality, and harmonizes thoughts and energetic patterns.

Cleansing Gemstone Jewelry

Because gems and minerals work their magic through vibration and energy, they can benefit from periodic cleansings, which clear negativity and harmonize vibrations and energetic patterns. If you haven't worn a piece for a while, you might like to cleanse it before wearing it. Another good time to cleanse your jewelry is after you've worn it for three days or so. However, if it's an especially absorbent crystal, such as moonstone or obsidian, you'll probably want to cleanse it daily. And if it possesses an exceptionally radiant or solid vibration (such as citrine quartz and diamonds do), you can cleanse it every couple of weeks to a month, or as your intuition dictates.

A simple way to cleanse your jewelry is by placing it in full sunlight (in a windowpane is fine) for at least a minute or two. Alternate ways are to run it under cold water, hold it in a moving body of water, or bathe it in sage smoke for a similar length of time.

Heirlooms

Provided your associations are positive, hand-me-downs from family members can represent and fortify our roots and can help activate the protection and guidance that we glean from our ancestors and family ties. For example, my dear friend Erin Jane Amabile relates:

> *My blue star necklace given to me by my grandmother, which had belonged to my great-grandmother before that, is my most cherished good luck charm. When I wear it, I like to imagine that I am activating a special connection to them. It makes me feel safe and strong.*

But even if your associations aren't totally positive, it's still possible that you can wear a piece handed down from your ancestors with positive magical results. For example, when my maternal grandmother died, my mom and aunt gave me her wedding ring. Everything I had heard about her marriage led me to believe that it was far from ideal, and other things my mom had told me (along with the fact that we hardly saw her or heard from her while she was alive) indicated that she was not particularly present or emotionally available. Still, the fact remains that she was my grandma: I carry her genes and her legacy. Before wearing her ring, I cleansed it with the intention to move her energy forward in the most positive of ways: to rise on her ashes with gratitude and love, and to transmute her challenges into wisdom. I perform a similar cleanse periodically and consider these intentions whenever I wear it. It's a bit different from Erin Jane's story, but it still connects me with my roots and lends me strength.

If you'd like to perform a cleanse like this on a particular piece, first check in with yourself to make sure that you feel good about this idea. If there is still a lot of old "stuff" leftover—i.e., if you're carrying around a lot of unresolved anger, pain, or unforgiveness related to the person who used to wear the piece—you might want to wait. On the other hand, your intuition might tell you that a cleansing like this might be just the thing to help you heal and emotionally evolve in the most desirable of ways. Bottom line: listen to your gut. Then, if you get the OK, you might want to perform one of the clearings here or devise something similar.

Heirloom Jewelry Clearing I: Sunlight

On the day of a full moon when the sky is clear and the sun is high in the sky, take the heirloom outside and lay it on a white cloth in the sunlight. While gazing at the piece, say:

> By the light of the sun, in all directions of
> time, all shadows depart, all challenges
> unwind, and all transforms into love.
>
> My roots go deep into the
> nourishing soil of the ages.
>
> Nourished by the strength and beauty of
> my ancestors, I rise with greater power,
> clarity, and wisdom than ever before.
>
> I am healthy, I am vibrant, I am whole.
> My way is clear, and all is well.
>
> Thank you, thank you, thank you.
> Blessed be. And so it is.

Allow the jewelry to soak up the sun for at least five more minutes as you send love and gratitude to the ancestors who have had the piece before you and to the entire family line.

Heirloom Jewelry Clearing II: Water

On the evening of a full moon when the moon is visible, take the piece to a clean, moving body of water: a river, a brook, a waterfall, or the sea. Hold it under the water for a minute or two, then hold it in your hand and bathe it in the light of the moon. Say:

> By the light of the moon, all negative
> patterns are now cleared from this piece and
> from my family in all directions of time.
>
> I glean wisdom from the past and move
> forward with confidence and joy.
>
> I connect with my roots in
> the healthiest of ways.
>
> I am healthy, I am vibrant, I am whole.
> My way is clear, and all is well.
>
> Thank you, thank you, thank you.
> Blessed be. And so it is.

Conjure up feelings of love and forgiveness for your ancestors and family line, then send these feelings into the jewelry as you continue to bathe it in the light of the moon. Feel the moonlight unraveling old issues and smoothing everything out. Stay with this for a minute or so or until the energy reaches a crescendo. It is done.

Pendants

When I was going to my very first author event, I stayed with my dad because the event wasn't far from my hometown. That morning, I asked him, "How do I look? Do I look like a metaphysical author?" After considering the question deeply and examining my outfit from head to toe, he declared simply, "You need a pendant."

Since then, I have noted on countless occasions that my father was correct in that pendants and metaphysical people seem to go hand in hand. If you want to see a bunch of really gorgeous pendants, go to a metaphysical conference. My theory is that those who are sensitive to energy agree that there is something particularly magical about a pendant. It's pretty much the only common jewelry piece that always sits at the center of your body, which is where your power centers (chakras) reside, and it normally rests over one of them, whether it's the throat, thymus, or heart chakra. Combined with the fact that a pendant is usually a gemstone or a symbol of some kind, this makes it a powerful amulet or charm, especially when selected and worn with intention.

So if you'd like to select a powerful pendant for a magical or metaphysical purpose, in addition to the previous gemstone section, check out the "Symbols" section in the "You Are a Guru" chapter. Then you can empower the pendant with a ritual like this one:

General Pendant Empowerment Ritual

On the evening of a full moon, light a white candle. (The color of the candle can be changed according to your intention; see the "Colors" section in the "You Are a Guru" chapter for ideas.) Cleanse your pendant in sage smoke. Dangle it a safe distance from the candle (so that it lights the pendant but doesn't burn it or otherwise compromise its appearance). Say something like, "I now empower this pendant with the energy of _____. As I wear it, I magnetize this condition in the most ideal of ways." If you like, you can also call on helpers of your choice to empower the pendant, such as angels, fairies, saints, or deities. Say, "Thank you, thank you, thank you. Blessed be. And so it is."

Pendant as Pendulum

In addition to all the magical powers of pendants alluded to above, pendants can double as pendulums. In other words, you can remove the pendant from your neck and use it as a divination device. To do so, you might want to research pendulums (there are a number of books on the subject, such as *Pendulum Magic for Beginners* by Richard Webster) or see if you have any luck with these basic instructions.

Cleanse a pendant in sage smoke or sunlight. Then, while holding it in your right hand, dangle it over your left hand. Wait until it stops swinging and is still. Then ask, "What is 'yes'?" Wait and see how the pendulum begins to move. It might move up and down, side to side, in a clockwise circle, or in a counterclockwise circle. Make a mental note of the way it moves. Then ask, "What is 'no'?" Again, see how it moves. Most likely, it will move in a different pattern than before. In the future, when you want to ask a yes or no question, remove the pendant from your neck and dangle it over your left hand in the same way. Wait until it's still, ask the question (silently or aloud), and observe the way it moves.

I have found that the most useful thing about pendulums is that they help us get in touch with what we already know but just don't know we know. In other words, our intuition and the subtle energy within our body knows a lot more than our logical, linear mind, such as what foods are the healthiest for us, what our heart of hearts really desires, where we put something that we have misplaced, or what choice or action might be the most nourishing to our well-being.

One
of my
favorite necklaces
is made from lovely
pale lavender stones with a
pink Kwan Yin...It always serves
as a reminder to be compassionate
and loving towards myself and others.

Rachel Avalon, holistic health coach and eco-expert

Ritual Adornment

An ancient Vedic philosophy states that it's important for a woman to contain and amplify her own Shakti/ life force/internal energy. This allows her to magnetize what she wants so that she's vital and radiant. One of the ritualized ways that women do this is to decorate themselves in the following ways:

- *a bindi (a gem or small decoration at the third eye) or, alternatively, a daily anointing of the third eye with essential oil or consecrated oil*
- *a piercing in your left nostril*
- *bracelets around your wrists*
- *anklets around your ankles*
- *a pendant on the heart chakra*
- *a pendant on the solar plexus chakra*
- *a hip chain that hangs to your sacral chakra*

I don't do all of that, but I anoint my third eye every day, I got my nostril pierced, and I wear the two necklaces. I interchange the pendants, but they always have a certain significance to me, whether it's because of a crystal, a symbol, or a precious metal.

SEDONA SOULFIRE, SACRED DANCER AND PRIESTESS

Earrings

Because they are on either side of your head, earrings have a unique ability to affect your thought processes and degree of clarity, and also to activate and enhance the energy centers near the top of your body, namely the throat, brow, and

You Are Ador(n)able

crown chakras. For example, if you're giving a presentation, you might want to wear longer earrings with a gemstone that enhances communication in order to activate your throat chakra. Or if you'd like to stay focused for a test, you might wear white quartz earrings (or another gemstone that facilitates clear thinking, such as fluorite). To activate inspiration and keep you connected with the Great Mystery (God/Goddess/All That Is), you could wear studs of something like amethyst or gold. You can also empower your earrings with your intention, perhaps with an adapted version of the previous general pendant empowerment ritual.

Adorning the Hands

Before we go into the various ways you can decorate your hands, keep in mind that hands are an emanation of the very bright and powerful energy center that resides in the center of our sternum: the heart chakra. This means that whether we are employing them to help us write, gesture, sew, paint, caress, pray, or anything else, hands are a means of expressing, projecting, and receiving emotions—ideally loved-based ones.

When you'd like to decorate your hands with accessories for the purpose of consciously affecting the quality of heart energy that you express and receive, keep in mind:

- The left hand receives and the right hand projects. The left hand emphasizes femininity and the right hand, masculinity. Adorning one or the other can help you emphasize the polarity that will most serve your intentions for the day. (See the

"You Are a Guru" chapter for more on polarity.) Although if you like a ring, and it just happens to fit well on a certain finger, that's another good reason to wear it on that finger. It's interesting to note the finger's connotations, though, as they will still be significant.

- The thumb represents intellect, analysis, judgement, confidence, and will. Consider how a "thumbs up" gesture—one or two—can symbolize a positive assessment, approval, or an infusion of strength and confidence (as in "everything's A-OK" or "you can do it"). A ring on the thumb can increase powers of discernment and clear judgment while infusing the wearer with confidence, determination, and personal power.

- The index finger represents projecting love outward into the world in the form of projects and expression. Wearing a ring on this finger can increase your ability to focus your love like a laser beam for the purpose of healing and bringing heart-centered goals into form in the physical world.

- The middle finger represents passion, sexuality, and righteous (warranted) anger. Wearing a ring on this finger can help you explore and express your anger in healthy ways, and it can help you feel more comfortable expressing your sexual self.

- The ring finger represents receiving love. As whoever began the wedding and engagement ring traditions must have known or sensed, wearing a ring on this finger can help you open your heart and let yourself be loved.

- The little finger represents loving communication as well as being in a loving and healthy relationship with your inner child. Wearing a ring on this finger can enhance your creativity, playfulness, and spontaneity, and it also can help facilitate clear communication with your loved ones.

- The wrist represents your personal flexibility and flow with regards to the ways that you give, receive, and express love. Wearing a bracelet helps with intentions related to flowing through the changes of your life with ease or opening up to the feminine qualities of receptivity and grace.

- Going accessory-free, yet keeping your hands clean and moisturized, can be a way to cleanse and simplify your emotions and emotional expression, and to clear the way for giving and receiving love, especially when you set that intention while concentrating on the flow of energy from your heart to your hands.

Rings

The unbroken circle of a ring is particularly suited to magical intentions that involve binding and commitments. For example, wedding and engagement rings indicate a lifelong commitment as well as the symbolic binding of one person to another. Additionally, unbroken circles (such as rings) are useful in magic involving protection.

Ring Protection Ritual

Choose a ring that feels protective to you. It might depict a protective symbol, contain a protective gemstone, or simply be a perfect silver or gold circle (which is protective in itself). On the full moon, light a white candle. Bathe the ring in white sage smoke. Set it on a white dinner plate, and surround it with a circle of sea salt. Direct your palms toward the ring as you say, "I now call on the great Mother Goddess. Please infuse this ring with the powerful energy of protection. May the wearer of this ring be surrounded in a circle of light in which only love remains and through which only love may enter. Thank you, thank you, thank you. Blessed be. And so it is." Visualize the ring surrounded in very bright, golden-white light. Continue visualizing this until the ritual feels complete. Extinguish the candle. Leave the ring in the salt ring overnight, then flush the salt down the toilet the next day.

Bracelets

Bracelets can be worn on the left wrist to enhance femininity or to help heal issues related to female family members or female sexuality, on the right wrist to enhance masculinity or to help heal issues related to male family members or male sexuality, or on both wrists at once for general protection and personal power.

When choosing bracelets for any of these intentions, tune in to the appearance and feel of the bracelet to make sure that it possesses the energy you're looking for. For example, sparkly, colorful bangles or delicate bracelets would enhance

I have this checker-print bracelet I bought in Costa Rica. I specifically got it because every time I see checker print, I think of Raver J [the comic book character I created], because that's part of the racer outfit I originally dressed her in—the black and the white symbolize mystery and purity. I'll wear it or place it on my altar when I'm channeling energy into finishing a project, to stay focused and to keep myself aligned with the character.

JANINE JORDAN

femininity, while cuff bracelets would be more likely to feel more masculine, protective, and empowering. Symbols, colors, and gemstones will also lend their particular vibes to the mix. Once you've selected the bracelet(s) that feel powerful for your magical purpose, you might adapt the general pendant empowerment ritual to empower it/them with your intention. Bracelets can also be good general talismans, like pendants.

Nail Polish

As emanations of the powerful energy at our heart, and as the symbols and actual tools of receiving, doing, and creating, hands are very powerful things. And, as the ten tips of these powerful energy centers in our bodies, our fingernails can be intentionally employed for magical purposes related to these intentions (receiving, doing, and creating). For example:

Red nail polish can be employed as an activator: paint your nails red with the intention of energizing and empowering your goals and your degree of success.

Gold nail polish can help you receive and generate wealth.

Green nail polish can enhance your heart chakra and your power to give and receive love.

Silver nail polish can activate your receptivity, intuition, and alignment with the moon.

Light or medium blue nail polish can facilitate written or typed communications.

Feet symbolize understanding and grounding, and toe-nail polish can be intentionally employed to help you connect with Mother Earth, enhance understanding of a particular issue, ground you in a particular energy, or generally gain your balance. For example:

Brown toenail polish can help you feel grounded and calm.

Green toenail polish can help you feel centered in wealth and abundance.

Red toenail polish can enhance your personal power and connect you with your roots.

Silver toenail polish can help you feel balanced, receptive, and serene.

Black toenail polish can help absorb excess energy and calm anxiety.

(For more color correspondences, see the "You Are a Guru" chapter.)

If you're on the daring side when it comes to your nail color choices, you can emphasize the associations with a particular finger by painting that finger a different color than the other fingers. You might do this on one or both hands, keeping in mind the associations of the left with receptivity/femininity and the right with projection/masculinity.

It should be noted also that at the time of this writing, nail art seems to be more popular than it's been in recent years. If you're a fan of the trend, you might like to consider the magical correspondences of fingers, hands, and the symbols or patterns you choose. Indeed, when chosen and applied with intention, nail art has the potential to be a very magical thing.

Tattoos

Granted, tattoos are not for everyone, so go ahead and skip this section if you're not a tattoo enthusiast and don't foresee becoming one. But if you're interested in this topic, I'm glad you're reading this, because the permanence of tattoos makes it especially important to be aware of the metaphysical connotations and dynamics of the design and placement that you choose, as well as the whole process of getting a tattoo.

First of all, I got all three of my tattoos years ago, way before I knew this, but I have recently been informed that tattoo ink often contains animal fat and bones. So you vegans and vegetarians out there will want to make a point of seeking out vegan tattoo ink.

Now that I've gotten that important tidbit out of the way, let's talk about choosing what you want to display on your body for the rest of your life. With all three of my tattoos, the idea for them arose organically in my mind, and I simultaneously felt something that can best be described as a craving for them to appear on a precise location on my body. It was like I couldn't rest until the thing I was imagining came into form in the physical world. Interestingly, my friend Erin Jane had a very similar experience:

All of my tattoos (four in all) are in places where I had a very distinct feeling that I needed to have a tattoo right there. A lot of times that feeling would come long before I even knew what I wanted the tattoo to be of. I would get an insatiable urge to feel the tattoo gun on those particular spots for some reason.

Considering that neither Erin nor I have ever regretted any of our tattoos, I feel that it's important to wait until the tattoo chooses you. Much like choosing who to marry (another decision with, ideally, lifelong implications), if you don't experience an inner nudging that tells you that you must definitely do so immediately, don't get a tattoo.

Of course, before you get a specific vision, you might have a general idea that you'd like to get a tattoo, at which time kicking around ideas, checking out artwork and other people's tattoos (online or in real life), and researching symbolism might be a good idea. Just let it all simmer in your mind like a cauldron until something definite arises out of the brew. And if it doesn't, hey! No problem—no tattoo today.

Lastly, find an artist that you really vibe with. You'll want not only to be an enthusiastic fan of his or her work, but also to really like him or her personally—because that person's energy is going to be literally under your skin for the rest of your life. My third and favorite tattoo was done by a really memorable woman with bright pink hair and an awesome sense of humor. What's more, she wouldn't sign off on my idea because she thought it was too boring, so she insisted that I select more colors than I had originally

You Are Ador(n)able

I felt like I
was having a Kundalini
experience while I was
getting the butterfly tattoo on
my back—like rushing sensations
from my tailbone and all the way up
my spine. Afterwards, I felt more like
myself and more comfortable in my skin.
Same with my nose piercing! It was
just like, "Uh, yeah, of course!"

SEDONA SOULFIRE,
SACRED DANCER AND PRIESTESS

You Are Ador(n)able

planned. She also made it so that the tattoo lies perfectly on my wrist. And it's a goddess symbol, so it's great that a powerful female was the one to do it.

Piercings

Acupuncture draws on the energy flows, or meridians, that move throughout the human body. In a similar way, piercings can activate and enhance our personal energy flow for specific purposes. In India, for example, women often get their noses pierced on the left side to enhance their feminine energy—you know, their curvy, receptive, magnetic allure. Other popular piercing locations and their energetic connotations include:

Right nostril: masculine energy (projection, assertiveness, action)

Left eyebrow: intuition, inner knowing

Right eyebrow: wisdom, self trust

Earlobes: focus, clarity

Right earlobe: communication, clear seeing

Left earlobe: comprehension, intuition

Right upper ear: balance, stress relief

Left upper ear: relaxation and sleep

Bellybutton: personal power, sexuality, creativity

Tongue, nipples, genitals: there are some exceptional health risks involved with these piercings, so I'm not going to endorse them here. I'm not saying don't pierce these areas; I'm just saying that if you do, you're on your own.

You Are Ador(n)able

Handbags and Wallets

Handbags and wallets are symbolic of wealth, both because they literally hold your cash and other payment options, and because they have the potential to add a look or feeling of affluence to your ensemble. For this reason, it's important to choose a handbag and wallet that enhance your feeling of wealth in some way, whether it's due to its color, material, pattern, or general appearance. For example, you might choose a handbag that looks like something a rich person would carry, or simply a handbag that is a shade of green that makes you think of wealth and abundance. Additionally, you might like to choose a red wallet to activate your finances, a black wallet to facilitate financial flow, a green wallet to generally magnetize prosperity, or a purple wallet to keep you in the vibration of wealth. A wallet that makes it easy for you to find things and get to them quickly will enhance your sense of ease around money, and consequently will provide a boost to your financial flow.

It's also ideal to select a handbag that matches what you're up to. Generally speaking, larger handbags are more ideal for daytime use, and smaller ones (like clutches or little sparkly purses) better suit nighttime activities. Furthermore, choose casual when you're doing something casual and dressy when you're doing something dressy. (Read: maybe don't go for a chichi purse with sweats or a sporty tote with stilettos.) Much like shoes, handbags really set the overall tone of your appearance and vibe.

It should also be noted that while in times past, matching your shoes and your handbag was a must, these days the etiquette is much more lax on this point. However, I find that it's good to be aware of this rule, just to make sure that your shoes and handbag are singing an energetic and aesthetic duet.

9

you are DIVINE

Consider for a moment one of the beings (human or animal) that you love the very most in the world. See yourself gazing into the eyes of this precious, dearly beloved creature. Feel your belly relax and your heart open as you connect with their heart. In your mind's eye, pull them close.

What did this being do to inspire this infinite, incomprehensible love? Perhaps they are adorable, perhaps they are sweet, perhaps they are always there for you when you need them. But what exactly is it about them that elicits such deep devotion? The answer is love itself. The divine spark that is your soul recognizes the divine spark that is their soul, and this opens you up to the endless sea of love that is the eternal truth behind the transient appearance of this earthly existence.

This spark of love that you recognize within this being is within you: it is the truth of who you are. You are an eternal,

> How is it
> possible that a being
> with such sensitive jewels
> as the eyes, such enchanted
> musical instruments as the ears,
> and such fabulous arabesque of
> nerves as the brain can experience
> itself anything less than a god?
>
> ALAN WATTS, PHILOSOPHER

divine being made from pure love and incarnated in a temporary earthly existence. You are a ray emanating from the One Divine Light, briefly illuminating the stage of time.

Occupying the border between seen and unseen, temporary and eternal, and animated with the light of infinite love, our bodies are literally living, breathing altars to the Divine. And when our actions are grounded in an awareness of our true divine nature, dressing, adorning, and caring for our bodies takes on a whole new energy. Like burning incense or offering flowers to a beloved deity, each becomes a way to express devotion, to connect with the infinite, and to honor the miraculous experience of being present in this physical world.

The Joy of Self-Care

[God] does not envy the soul so much.

He is all soul

but He would like to house it in a body

and come down

and give it a bath

now and then.

There have been times in my life when I have thought of self-care as just one more thing on the to-do list. And there have even been times when I have had to fight strong undercurrents of self-loathing during my self-care practices, such as when I showered, put on makeup, or took care of my skin. But now, as much as I possibly can, I look forward to it and think of it as a joyful privilege and art form.

One way to think of your body is like a wind chime that divine wind wants to whisper through or like a stained-glass window that the divine sunlight wants to illuminate. When you take the time to tune your chime or buff your window, your divine beauty can sing or radiate through in the most ideal way. In fact, because a precept of metaphysics is that energy flows where attention goes, the mere act of taking a good look at your skin and lovingly tending to it in exactly the way it needs to be tended to—just the energy behind the act, not even the products or techniques you use—will soothe stress and add brightness and magnetism to your energy field. This is why, after a couple of hours at the spa or after taking a good, satisfying shower, we feel not just

205
· · ·
You Are Divine

clean and beautiful in a physical way, but also luminous and lovable in a spiritual way.

Hair

Hair is like a mantle of power, a unique cloak or personal radiance all your own. Caring lovingly for your hair can support your feelings of self-confidence and self-love, or—as author and *Glamour* beauty editor Andrea Pomerantz Lustig calls it—"hair happiness." Additionally, according to ancient Chinese wisdom, like a flowing fountain near the entrance quadrant in your home, a head of soft, splendorous hair supports the degree of your financial well-being. (Although loving your hair exactly as it is can be just as powerful!)

If it feels right, when you comb, brush, or otherwise care for your hair, you might inwardly recite a devotional mantra such as: "As I brush my hair, I express loving devotion to the God/dess within. I radiate divine power, I radiate divine grace. I am a clear and potent channel of divinity." Or, for a simpler option, you might just approach the whole act in a reverent way.

While everyone's hair is different, it's important to find a hair-care regimen that works for you. Also be sure to pay attention to the health of your scalp, which has everything to do with the integrity of your hair. If your hair tends to be dry or has been damaged by styling or the sun, you might want to consider incorporating a regular (perhaps weekly) deep conditioning treatment. For a simple, natural one, mash or blend an avocado, then blend in a few drops of lavender essential oil. Gently massage into your scalp and saturate each section of your hair, down to the ends. Wrap in plastic and leave on for twenty minutes, then rinse.

You might also want to consider choosing a color and style to enhance your elemental makeup and intentions. For example:

- Brightening highlights and red tones, as well as wild or eye-catching styles, enhance the fire element and fuel intentions related to fame and socializing.

- Warm gold and brown tones, as well as traditional or conventional styles, enhance the earth element and intentions related to family and nurturing.

- Ash, platinum, or gray tones, as well as sleek styles, enhance the metal element and intentions related to thought and precision.

- Black and very dark brown tones, as well as long and flowing styles, enhance the water element and intentions related to writing, art, and emotions.

- Natural and light brown tones, as well as effortless and sporty styles, enhance the wood element and intentions related to self-improvement and exercise.

Find a colorist you like or do it yourself if you're experienced or just plain brave. (But for heaven's sake, be careful!) And while I tend to believe that everyone is entitled to the hair color that they most authentically desire, I also strongly suggest finding the most natural and cruelty-free options possible.

Skin

Skin is literally the border between us and the outside world. As such, it can mirror our sensitivity to outside conditions and stimuli. I've thought a lot about this because in the past, my skin has reacted violently to mysterious allergens or has been prone to various types of breakouts. I believe that when this has happened, I felt—in some capacity—unsafe, unprotected, and threatened. Either that, or I could have been processing old "stuff" that was coming to the surface to be seen and then be released. I have considered the phrases "under my skin" and "uncomfortable in my skin" and found that one or both of these might be at work when my skin is not at its best. I also find my sensitive skin to be a mirror of my sensitivity and intuitiveness in general, so, just as I have to be very careful to care for and shield my energetic body and emotions because of my innate sensitivity, I find that I have to be very careful with my skin.

In addition to serving as a diagnostic tool for inner conditions and as a possible indicator of outer conditions that we may not be totally comfortable with, we can draw upon the power of our skin to help us feel grounded in a feeling of safety and support. (As in the phrase "thick skinned" or the converse of the above-mentioned phrase about being "comfortable in one's skin.") As a result, we also feel confident. This, combined with the visual clarity and beauty of our skin, results in an enhanced level of radiance.

Just like with hair, everyone's skin is different, so there is no one regimen that will work for everyone. Still, to care for both the physical and energetic aspects of your skin, you might consider:

- drinking lots of water (this is pretty much always a good idea)

- moisturizing with a natural oil or gentle lotion

- exfoliating your face weekly or biweekly (coffee grounds or baking soda both work as a good exfoliation ingredient for some people, though they may be too harsh for some)

- taking liver-cleansing supplements or drinking herbal tea containing herbs such as milk thistle, red clover blossom, dandelion root, or burdock (although it's a good idea to take breaks from herbs or to cycle them out of your regimen periodically)

- taking probiotics

- doing breathing exercises or "pranayam" as part of a yoga practice or alone

- eating lots of raw fruits and vegetables, especially leafy greens—another one that's basically a good idea for everyone

- getting lots of sleep

- lovingly attending to your skin; as you bathe or moisturize, you might repeat a mantra inwardly such as, "I love and approve of myself. I am safe and protected. All is well."

⁓ Skin RX Visualization ⁓

If sensitive skin, acne, or another persistent skin condition seems to be a problem, sit comfortably, relax your body, and take some deep breaths. Then visualize a vacuum tube of light vacuuming all negative and unpleasant energies out of your aura and chakras. Follow up by visualizing a globe of protective, very bright golden-white, peachy pink, or light aquamarine light (choose the one that feels most powerful) completely surrounding your body and aura, protecting and shielding you from all that is not love and transmuting all negative energies into positive ones. (Repeat as desired, but perhaps refresh every twenty-four hours or so. Also be sure to drink lots of water.)

For me,
scrubbing
my face and body
with a homemade
salt scrub achieves two
things; first, it reveals a smooth,
fresh glow, and second, the act of
sloughing off old dead skin feels like a
renewal of the self beyond the physical.
ERIN JANE AMABILE, MAGICAL FASHIONISTA

Mouth

In Chinese face reading, the mouth symbolizes one's degree of prosperity, so luscious, moisturized lips and gleaming, healthy teeth help support a luxurious inflow of wealth and resources. When you think about it, this makes sense, since this is the place where we receive our nourishment from the outside world and it's the place where we express our degree of happiness (in the form of a smile). In a parallel way, the appearance and health of this area symbolizes our degree of well-being, as well as the quality of energy that we are drawing into our lives.

Knowing this makes shopping for lip balm and toothpaste seem even more fun, doesn't it? And it also makes flossing seem a little bit less mundane and a little bit more essential.

To have even more fun with it, you might consider:

- choosing a lip balm that's scented with a wealth-drawing herb or scent such as peppermint, vanilla, or tangerine

- wearing any shade of red lipstick, as red is a wealth- and happiness-drawing color

- wearing a tastefully glistening or slightly wet-looking lip gloss. The appearance of moisture represents the water element, which represents nourishment and affluence—although at this stage in the lip gloss trend, too much glossiness can start to cause one to resemble a tacky porn star, so be aware.

Eyes

Not only are the eyes our window to the appearance of the world around us, but the eyes are also, proverbially, "the window to the soul." In other words, they represent both the way we see the world and the way the world sees us. That's why, when I'm feeling particularly vulnerable but for some reason still need to traverse some region of the bustling city in which I live, I throw on some dark glasses. Then I feel a little bit more of a cushion: even though I can still see the world and the world can still see me, I feel both shielded and hidden.

Other ways to work with the energy of your eyes include:

- keeping the area around your eyes moisturized (I really like DermaE Pycnogenol Eye Gel, but find one that works for you)

- applying tasteful eye makeup with intention— you might (for example) set the intention to see prosperity everywhere you look or see everyone and everything with the eyes of love; as you apply your makeup, you can then recite your intention as an affirmation

- darkening or enhancing your eyebrows; this will lend authority to your presence

- reducing or lightening your eyebrows; this will soften your presence and reduce your tendency to want to be in control

- shaping (or plucking the regrowth) around your eyebrows; this will hone your focus and help clarify your personal vision

- wearing a pair of glasses that help you
  to feel the way you want to feel: fun,
  intelligent, hip, adventurous, wealthy, etc.

Hands

As we touched on in the previous chapter, you might say
that hands are the heart in action. The energy of love flows
powerfully from our hearts, down our arms, and into our
hands. This is why hugging or holding hands feels like a
natural thing to do when we want to express love. To further illustrate, consider that:

- "handmade with love" feels like a natural phrase

- we clench our hands when we are feeling
  something we don't want to be feeling

- just placing a hand on someone's shoulder can
  infuse them with feelings of support

- we talk with our hands when we especially want
  to express a feeling

- rings can be among the most sentimental variety
  of jewelry

- "extending a helping hand" is a gesture of loving
  action

Attentively caring for and adorning our hands can affect
the way we express our love in the world and the ways that
others perceive this expression. Moisturized and manicured
hands allow love and healing energy to flow unimpeded out
from our hearts and into the world, whether it's in the form
of typing or writing words that are expressions of love (as I

am doing now), drawing, painting, sewing, cleaning, petting the cat, hugging your child, baking cookies, or healing your partner's headache with Reiki or healing touch.

Then again, hands that are simply clean and well-cared-for can be great too, and there's no need to go all-out if manicured paws aren't your thing. Personally, I go through phases. (For jewelry and manicure ideas, see the previous chapter.)

Feet

Our feet are the connection point between us and our divine Mother Earth. Soaking our feet or getting a foot massage helps remind us of this primal connection and our divine heritage, as does adorning our feet in delightful shoes. Indeed, I believe every shoe lover will agree that wearing a pair of shoes that we adore can feel like offering a fragrant bouquet on an altar to our own divine nature.

Similarly, a simple way to get grounded and to activate your sensuality and feeling of physical well-being is just to take a moment to rub lotion into your feet. Add a few drops of essential oil to the lotion to increase the effect. For example, you might try:

- patchouli for extra earth energy and sensuality

- peppermint for invigoration

- lavender for stress relief

- geranium for PMS relief and hormone balance

Stand Like a Celebrity

Once you get the hang of it, it feels wonderful and natural to stand with relaxed shoulders, your heart open, your torso and belly elongated, and your hips tilted back—perhaps even with one hip jutting out and one of your relaxed hands resting on your hip? Try it. If you want a visual, look at a picture of almost anyone standing on a red carpet. Believe it or not, once you master this stand, you'll look slimmer, your clothes will hang better, and you'll appear younger, more vital, and more charismatic. Not only that, but when we move and stand like we're utterly confident, we begin to feel utterly confident almost immediately. And did I mention this posture even helps your digestion? Experiment with this a little, and you'll see that what I'm telling you is true.

If it feels totally weird to you at first, I suggest doing at least a little bit of yoga daily to enhance your posture, and also putting on your playlist from chapter one and doing huge hip circles to increase the range of motion in your hips and to increase the familiarity of free and fluid movement in the hip area. Just take a little bit of time to stand with your feet apart and knees slightly bent. Then slowly push your hips in huge circles, as far as they'll go in every direction. Imagine that you are stirring a huge cauldron with your hips. Then switch and do the circles the other way.

Walk Like a Supermodel

Speaking of hips, confident movement, and feeling fabulous inside and out—you know what else is fun? Walking. I think the most entrancing thing about the way that supermodels

During my meditation or as I'm going to sleep, I scan my body to get in touch with it and feel the sensations of having a physical form. I try to get deeper and deeper, to the deepest cellular level, and then I send a huge amount of love to the physical matter of my body, just for being here for me—you know, for being half of the equation of this life experience that I'm having. It's essentially a process of marrying my physical body to my soul self. Because really, what's not to love about your body? It's doing all these miraculous functions at all times! It's a sparkling reflection of the cosmic intelligence, this amazing manifestation of divinity! Why would I ever have thought negatively about it or had self-defeating thoughts about it? I'm working hard to undo all that old programming right now.

SEDONA SOULFIRE, SACRED DANCER AND PRIESTESS

walk when they're on the catwalk is that they aren't walking to get anywhere: they are walking to walk. The walking is the destination. Because they are present with each step, the observer feels compelled not just by their beauty but also their mystery, confidence, and allure. But all of that aside, walking to walk is just plain fun, like dancing. Plus, you're going to walk anyway, so why not have fun with it?

Here are some tips for how to have fun with your walk and to look great all the while:

- Think to yourself: "How can I really enjoy walking from here to there?"

- Swing your hips and let them feel open, fluid, and relaxed. Let your body move like it wants to move, and if feelings of shame or fear come up as you do this, just remind yourself (again and again if you have to) that it's okay to enjoy being in your body! Our culture has evolved a lot in the last few hundred years. Nowadays, it's very unlikely that someone is going to burn you at the stake for being sexy and free.

- If you're not in a hurry, don't hurry. If you are in a hurry, are you really? If so, you can still enjoy walking—just walk a little faster.

- Enjoy the feeling of each footfall as it connects to the receptive and nourishing energy of the earth.

- Enjoy the beauty of the world around you.

- Enjoy the feeling of breeze on your skin and your hair on your neck.

- Keep your shoulders back and torso elongated. Again, you might want to add a little yoga to your daily regimen if this feels weird at first.

- Notice where you're holding tension, and relax it. Some common areas where people hold tension include the jaw, neck, shoulders, belly, hips, and knees. Do neck circles, conscious breathing, or light stretching if necessary to help yourself let that tension go.

General Health and Beauty Guidelines

As we touched on in the skin section above, enhancing your beauty in a holistic, inside-out sort of way is really the best and most potent cosmetic. So, in addition to approaching the whole subject with joy, reverence, and self-love, it's important to keep the following guidelines in mind.

Exercise

In addition to burning calories and helping us stay healthy, exercise gets our blood pumping, energizes our mind, reduces stress, and increases our oxygen intake—all very important beauty factors. So find something you like, and do it daily (or, as I like to say, almost daily; I shoot for daily, but it doesn't always work out that way).

Be sure to switch it up if it gets boring. It's more important to exercise on a consistent basis than to kick your butt every day, so take it easy if you're not in the mood for a crazy workout some days.

Meditate, Breathe, and Relax

Despite how much we may be doing in the external world, experiencing luxurious relaxation at our core really is that certain something that lends radiance and irresistible allure to our presence. So a daily meditation practice (even a five-minute one!) can make all the difference. You might just play some relaxing music and watch your breath as it goes in and out, or visualize yourself being bathed in white light as you consciously relax each muscle and muscle group. Again, it's more important that you do it than how you do it. Even if you just sit there for five minutes with nothing else you're supposed to be doing, that's better than nothing, and it's a great way to get the snowball of a lifelong habit to initiate its proverbial roll down the hill.

Also, as mentioned above, throughout the day, take a moment to notice where you're tensing up and consciously relax that area, along with your entire body. Similarly, notice your breath as it goes in and out, and allow it to consciously deepen. You normally hear this type of advice for the purpose of aligning with your spirituality and reducing stress—which you are definitely doing!—but let's not forget that you are also enhancing your attractiveness and charm in a serious way.

Get Enough Sleep

Every time I think of beauty sleep, I think of Miss Piggy, one of many beauty icons for whom it was so important. (Am I the only one who always equates the two?) My rule of thumb is at least seven hours, but eight is my ideal.

Still, everyone's different, so find what works for you. It's also helpful to find your best sleep schedule and, generally speaking, stick to it. (Excepting those moments when you must take an early flight or when you feel drawn to shine your divine radiance on the dance floor or at a royal gala of some sort, of course.)

If you have trouble sleeping, make sure you're exercising regularly, and make sure your bedroom is clean, relaxing, and free of clutter. (You might also try covering any mirrors to see if that helps.) If you still have trouble sleeping, cut back on caffeine and don't eat anything substantial for at least three hours before bed. Next thing to try: drink chamomile tea (or a blend such as Sleepytime) and diffuse lavender essential oil in your bedroom just before bed. If that also doesn't work, try taking kava and valerian supplements, separately or together.

For you overachievers, here are a few enhancements to beauty sleep that you might want to consider trying:

- put a heavy moisturizer on your hands, cover them with cotton gloves, and leave on overnight

- sleep on your back to minimize lines on your face, neck, and décolletage

- remove your makeup and—if your skin seems to want it—apply a night cream to your face and neck before bed

Soak

I love baths! Soaking in a hot bath into which I've dissolved about ½ to ¾ cup sea salt not only moisturizes my skin, it also cleanses and detoxifies my body and aura, relaxes my muscles, and melts away my stress. Plus, I've noticed that for about twenty-four hours after I take a hot bath, I look younger *and* I get more compliments than usual on my skin.

Other fun things you might add to your bath experience include:

- candles

- incense

- white or green tea bags (then place them on your eyes as you soak to reduce puffiness)

- rose petals

- ¼ cup baking soda to lift your spirits

- an aromatherapy blend in a diffuser

- 1 cup Epsom salts to relax your muscles and detoxify

- 1 cup finely ground rolled oats (use a coffee grinder until they are a fine powder)—this is great for itchy skin, sensitive skin, or eczema

Also, be sure to drink plenty of water as you soak to replenish your fluids and help move toxins out of your body. Oh, and don't let your hair soak in salt water, as that dries it out. In fact, you might want to shower afterwards so that you can wash and condition your hair.

Choose Beautifying Foods and Beverages

For the beauty-conscious individual, raw veggies and fruit (especially organic) are where it's at! They're filled to the brim with antioxidants, moisture, enzymes, and life-force energy. Seriously, hoity-toity celebrity spa treatments and energy supplements both pale in comparison to the power of a raw veggie and fruit-rich diet.

I make it a
priority to have what
I like to call Mermaid Time.
That's when I take an Epsom
salt bath or go swimming. At the
very least, as a busy mom, I'll just
take a hot shower and breathe in some
essential oils like bergamot, douglas fir,
peppermint, or geranium, depending
on the season and my mood.

RACHEL AVALON, HOLISTIC HEALTH COACH
AND ECO-EXPERT

Even though I don't practice every single suggestion in Kimberly Snyder's book *The Beauty Detox Solution*, I do practice a number of them, and perhaps my favorite is to always eat raw, fresh vegetables before you eat anything else. So, to give you an idea of what this looks like for me, I eat a bowl of plain raw baby spinach as soon as I get up in the morning. (It's actually pretty pleasant and goes by very quickly—I don't know why everyone doesn't do it!) Then I have a bit of breakfast, such as almonds or fruit. For lunch, I'll often have a plate of raw veggies (such as carrots, bell peppers, and cucumbers), some of which I dip in a mix of salsa and hummus, though I like the carrots plain. Then I might have a main course, such as a vegan bran muffin or a bit of grilled tofu (unless I'm going all raw, which I sometimes do). At dinner, I'll have a couple of carrots or some cucumbers before I have something like rice or quinoa and some grilled veggies, or maybe some vegan Indian food. Throughout the day I'll snack on fresh or dried fruit if I get hungry, and I do my best to drink plenty of water. And then, after a day of eating so shockingly well, I'll sometimes happily enjoy some dark chocolate, organic black licorice, or vegan cookies. Even though I regularly change my diet in small ways to keep it fresh, and even though I have sometimes in the past found myself spiraling into slightly less stellar habits, the eating routine I described above is a good example of my ideal, some incarnation of which I make a habit of returning to again and again.

In addition to generally eating lots of veggies and fruit, and drinking lots of water, you might keep in mind that the following foods and beverages are considered by many nutritionists to be especially beautifying:

- almonds

- avocados

- leafy greens

- berries

- probiotic supplements or foods containing probiotics such as soy or coconut yogurt

- blended drinks made with berries and lots of leafy greens

- fresh veggie juice

- pomegranate juice

- cucumbers

- green tea

Take a Break from Your Undergarments

Like so many of us, I love a good underwire bra and a sexy pair of panties. Still, underwire bras, and bras in general, can inhibit lymph circulation and, as a result, might contribute to breast cancer. Panties, especially ones made with synthetic fabric, may contribute to yeast infections by increasing heat and restricting oxygen flow. So, while I simply cannot part with my lovely underthings, I do my best to remove my bra when I'm at home (just like removing my shoes) and to choose cotton panties or go without them completely (with clean pajama pants or a nightgown) whenever possible.

Protect from the Sun

Until I recently reached a certain age that shall remain nameless (okay: thirty-five), I really couldn't take the whole sunscreen thing seriously. But to the date of the above-mentioned birthday, I began acting like a vampire, wearing a sun hat and scarf every time I went in the sun and protecting every inch of my skin with super-strong sunscreen. Although I've eased up quite a bit in the weeks and months since that particular birthday, the whole thing is actually kind of fun. It's a way to treat myself like a treasured object or a priceless work of art. It also kind of makes me feel legitimately glamorous, like I'm a movie star.

It would also have been fun—and even more effective—if I had started earlier. But now is better than never. It really does look so lovely to have even-toned, sun-protected skin, and, as we've all heard a million times, it's invaluable for preserving your skin's smoothness and elasticity.

Speaking of which…

A Few Words on Aging

As with so many things fashion and beauty related, the French seem to have an enviable (and totally copyable) perspective on aging. Author Helena Frith-Powell writes, "Respect, admiration, and acceptance of age are nothing new to the French woman. Collette, the writer, was famous for having a string of young lovers who found her irresistible, even in her old age..." She goes on to describe how French women are less likely to get plastic surgery, as they see the wisdom that comes with aging as something that gives dimension to one's beauty, so they don't try to hide it as much as British and American women might. This sentiment is echoed by Sandrine Bernard, executive vice president of Solstiss (a high-end French lace manufacturer), who is quoted in *More Magazine* as saying, "French women are more relaxed about getting older, because it brings us another layer of knowledge about living...French women do not care about youth. They want to look natural."

Indeed, living in Los Angeles, I have to say that I see a lot of age-fighting going on, and when it's (literally) painfully obvious, it (literally) isn't pretty. As my friend Rachel points out, the term "pro-beauty" is a much more empowering term than "anti-aging." Take care of yourself, sure! Slather on that moisturizer, and don't go gray if you don't want to go gray! But don't assume that you need to fight your years or be ashamed of them in any way. Own them, and be proud of who you are, what you've learned, and how far you've come.

That doesn't mean, of course, that an eternally youthful spirit isn't something to continually cultivate. What people see when they encounter you, after all, isn't just how your makeup is done or how many wrinkles you have: it's your energy field and soul presence—the way you sparkle and flow. In fact, it might even be said that your subtle self is the most attractive thing about you. Here are some ideas for keeping the spirit youthful, buoyant, and expansive:

- stay inspired at all costs!

- read and study what interests you

- take classes or go on adventures that challenge you

- dance

- try new things

- be open to new ideas

- laugh hard

- be sensual and sexual, whether alone or with a partner

- read or watch erotica

- create art

- eat delicious things

- wear lovely undergarments

- give yourself treats

- do things that delight you

Author Sara Wiseman, in *The Four Passages of the Heart*, puts it beautifully when she says, "Your body is a divine container that will change over your lifetime. Revel in this! Notice it! This is the way of things: the softening of the shell so the soul may emerge." And Judith Sills, author of *Getting Naked Again*, says in *More Magazine*, "My attitude is, every passing year, get sexier, looser, have a better time, be out there more, dress for yourself more, speak for yourself more, flirt more, because who the hell cares anymore?"

Adorn and Care for Yourself Adoringly

What do I really feel like wearing today? What will enhance the feelings of self-love that I have for myself today? Do I really like this, or am I just telling myself that I should like it? Keeping in mind that I am a divinity and a masterpiece—and that this day is precious beyond comprehension—how shall I care for my body? This is the mindset with which to approach your closet, mirror, and self-care practices, not just for special occasions but every day. Let self-care and self-adornment be exercises in honoring your divinity and connecting with your truest, most authentic essence.

10

you are
PURE
INSPIRATION

We all wish for a satisfying creative outlet and an endlessly inspiring wellspring from which to regularly draw. I would suggest that our wardrobe and daily clothing choices offer both of these things every single day. By showing up consciously at our closets and allowing our choices to both mirror and fuel our feelings of enchantment, self-love, and love for the world around us, we bless ourselves daily with a nourishing infusion of joy.

This chapter provides suggestions for how to keep that inspiration alive and fresh, and how to continually express our unique essence through our clothing and self-care practices.

> Nothing is just what it seems: All things have a meaning beyond their purpose, and naught more so than clothes.
>
> TERESA MOOREY
> IN *THE FAIRY BIBLE*

Be Creative and Be Yourself

Just because you haven't seen anyone else do it—in your neighborhood or in the world—doesn't mean you shouldn't. If it sounds good, try it and see how it feels. Layer two sundresses on top of each other. Wear knee-high socks with your cutoffs. Tie a funky old tie around your sunhat. Someone, somewhere, starts every trend—it may as well be you! And even if you don't end up wearing it out of the house, trying it and parading in front of the mirror won't hurt a bit.

Also, if you still love the boots that some fashion magazine tells you are "so five years ago," screw 'em! What do they know?

As long as you feel great, and your gut tells you that you will continue to feel great when you walk outside your door and do whatever it is you're planning to do in that outfit, *wear the outfit*. As we have seen, it's your level of confidence and comfort in any given ensemble that gives it an aura of credibility and stylishness, not what some magazine says or what everyone else is doing that year.

As a matter of fact, some people—such as my friend Rachel Avalon (whom I have quoted throughout this book)—find it helpful to abstain from looking at fashion magazines altogether and to make a point of establishing more inclusive beauty standards. In her words:

> I recommend avoiding fashion magazines or shows that promote a narrow standard of beauty and overemphasize self-worth through trendy stuff. I also surround myself with amazing friends who are proactive in challenging the toxic norm and focusing on the joy and magic in life.

Find Inspiration Everywhere

Many fashion experts recommend gathering pictures of models and celebrities in outfits that you love so that you can keep the looks in mind when shopping and getting dressed. And this can be great fun, so go ahead and do it if you feel so inclined. But I would take this a step further and say this: don't just find inspiration from celebrities and models, find inspiration from everyone and everything. For example:

You might find inspiration from books. Last year, for example, I went through an old detective-novel phase and began wearing a trench coat. Similarly, after I go on a romance novel bender, I often can be found in a locket and a lot of frilly lace. And then sometimes, for an artful juxtaposition and if I'm feeling both hard-boiled and girly, I might wear the locket, the lace, *and* the trench coat.

You might find inspiration from movies. In the movie *Unzipped*, it's revealed that the designer Isaac Mizrahi is constantly inspired by various old movies. As he works on creating a line with tons of huge coats and faux fur, he constantly references the classic documentary *Nanook of the North*. Similarly, Tim Gunn's book *Tim Gunn: A Guide to Quality, Taste, and Style* includes a list of movies in the appendix that have particularly lent inspiration to his fashion journey.

Flaunt It

In the 1927 classic silent film It, *Clara Bow (a.k.a. the original "It" girl) plays a financially challenged sales clerk who falls for the ritzy boss of the department store where she works. A veritable lesson on confidence, mojo, and attracting the life of your dreams despite a limited wardrobe and limited funds (notice how she works sartorial magic with her sassy inventiveness), the movie is a must-see. Watch it and learn!*

"The possession of *It* must be absolutely unselfconscious and must have that magnetic 'sex appeal' which is irresistible..."
ELINOR GLYN, SCREENWRITER AND AUTHOR

You might find inspiration from nature. Perhaps a nasturtium will catch your eye in the springtime and you'll realize how lovely you'd feel in a bright orange scarf. Or maybe on your morning hike you're struck by the melancholy beauty of a regal deodar cedar, which initiates your search for a gauzy, forest-green shawl or a woodsy perfume.

You might find inspiration from artists. The designer Yves Saint Laurent was famously inspired by the artist Mondrian, with whom he also collaborated on a line of dresses. Similarly, if your appreciation of beauty finds itself fixated on a particular artist or painting, you might ask yourself how you can reflect and channel that beauty into your wardrobe choices.

You might find inspiration from mythology. Off and on for the last ten years or so, I've noticed the Greek-goddess look (drapy, light fabric with braided gold belts and other accessories evocative of pillars and togas) flow on and off of the red carpets. But every culture has mythology of some sort, so if, for example, you're presently fascinated by Lakshmi, the Hindu goddess of luxury and wealth, perhaps you can incorporate some pinks, yellows, and golds into your wardrobe, or even just a few jingly bangles. Or if you're feeling really daring and free, you might even wear a sparkly bindi at the center of your forehead. (Other mythological beings who lend themselves to fashion inspiration: mermaids, fairies, and nymphs.)

You might find inspiration in random places. In my little hometown in the central farmland of California, believe it or not, there is still a downtown drugstore with a soda fountain and sandwich counter. The women who work there wear pastel button-down shirts that are somehow evocative of both hospital scrubs and small-town waitress dresses. If you found yourself in my town having a peanut butter and jelly sandwich and a cherry phosphate, you might look at these women and think to yourself, "How cute would it be to wear one of those tops like a mini dress with a little belt and high-heeled boots?"—or maybe you would never think that in a million years. Either way, the point is that if you keep your eyes open to the world around you all the time, you will keep your wardrobe inspired and fresh, and you will also continually appreciate and feel inspired by the beauty and style that always surrounds you.

My
style
reflects my
past lives! My
wardrobe reflects an
Atlantean or Lemurian
time for sure. I also feel
a tie-in with ancient Egypt.
SEDONA SOULFIRE,
SACRED DANCER AND PRIESTESS

Be a Vessel of Appreciation for Others

Now that you're a fashion mystic, your eyes will be open to others in a new way. Every dimension of your hairdresser's face will suddenly tell you something about her innermost self. You'll see her interplay of elements and how she radiates her unique essence into the world. You might finally notice that she always wears a charm necklace with a little airplane pendant, and you might ask her, "Are you a pilot?" "Yes," she might say, "I just finally got my license. I've always wanted to fly." Then a whole new aspect of her beauty presents itself in your awareness as you consider her as a little girl gazing up, wide-eyed and wistful, at the clouds.

And instead of seeing others as more or less beautiful than you are, you'll see everyone as equally beautiful and equally deserving of love. Like going to a museum full of precious relics, simply going out in public will be an opportunity to appreciate the multifaceted, endlessly inspiring jewels that surround you in the form of people.

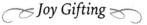

Joy Gifting

One way to enhance the joyful experience of your own—and everyone else's—beauty (which, by the way, will enhance your personal magnetism) is by practicing what author Carolyn Elliott calls "joy gifting." To do so, sit comfortably, close your eyes, and relax. When you feel ready, set a timer for five minutes and call to mind someone that you really like. Now begin to envision this person receiving all the gifts and experiencing all the conditions that will bring them the most joy. If you aren't sure what these are, pretend that you do. See them smiling and laughing as they experience more and more joy. When the timer dings, repeat this process three more times: with someone you kind of know or don't really know but know exists; then with someone you have trouble with, such as an enemy or mother-in-law; and then finally with yourself. If you practice this every day for a week, you will begin to feel your heart open more and more easily to everyone you meet, and life will feel much more satisfying and full. Once you experience these benefits firsthand, you may choose to continue the habit daily or as desired.

In an important way, each and every person's heart is brighter and more radiant than the sun. As you shine your own unique light generously while relaxing, breathing, and allowing yourself to perceive all of life as one dance of inspiration, it will feel natural to appreciate the light of others and to connect with them in a welcoming, loving way. Like a mirror reflecting the blinding sun, this loving interaction will always increase our own radiance and the overall radiance quotient in the world. Appreciate beauty, reflect beauty, express beauty, and be the pure beauty that you are. And please be assured that when you live this way, everyone benefits.

BIBLIOGRAPHY

Baumgartner, Jennifer. *You Are What You Wear: What Your Clothes Reveal About You*. Boston: De Capo, 2012.

Butler, Jennifer. *Reinventing Your Style: 7 Strategies for Looking Dynamic, Powerful, and Inspiring*. Los Angeles, CA: Jennifer Butler Living Color, 2007.

Cameron, Julia. *The Artist's Way: A Spiritual Path to Higher Creativity*. New York: Jeremy P. Tarcher, 1992.

Collins, Terah Kathryn. *The Western Guide to Feng Shui*. Carlsbad, CA: Hay House, 1996.

Connelly, Dianne M. *Traditional Acupuncture: The Law of the Five Elements*. Columbia, MD: Traditional Acupuncture Institute, 1979.

Cunningham, Scott. *Magical Aromatherapy: The Power of Scent*. St. Paul, MN: Llewellyn, 1989.

Dayan, Steven, MD. *Subliminally Exposed: Shocking Truths about Your Hidden Desires in Mating, Dating, and Communicating*. New York: Morgan James Publishing, 2013.

Deida, David. *Dear Lover: A Woman's Guide to Men, Sex, and Love's Deepest Bliss*. Louisville, CO: Sounds True, 2006.

Dugan, Ellen. *Seasons of Witchery: Celebrating the Sabbats with the Garden Witch*. Woodbury, MN: Llewellyn, 2012.

Elliott, Carolyn. *Awesome Your Life: The Artist's Antidote to Suffering Genius*. Ninety-Nine (Per)cent Press, 2011.

Frith-Powell, Helena. *All You Need to Be Impossibly French: A Witty Investigation into the Lives, Lusts, and Little Secrets of French Women*. New York: Plume, 2006.

Glamour Editors. "What the Experts Say." *1,000 Ways to Dress 10 Pounds Slimmer* (*Glamour* Special Edition). September 2012, 18–19.

Groover, Rachael Jayne. *Powerful and Feminine: How to Increase Your Magnetic Presence and Attract the Attention You Want*. Nampa, ID: Deep Pacific Press, 2011.

Gunn, Tim, and Kate Moloney. *Tim Gunn: A Guide to Quality, Taste, and Style*. New York: Abrams Image, 2007.

Gunn, Tim, and Ada Calhoun. *Tim Gunn's Fashion Bible*. New York: Gallery, 2012.

Haner, Jean. *The Wisdom of Your Face: Change Your Life with Chinese Face Reading!* Carlsbad, CA: Hay House, 2008.

Hay, Louise. *You Can Heal Your Life*. Carlsbad, CA: Hay House, 1984.

Hicks, Esther, and Jerry Hicks. *Ask and It Is Given*. Carlsbad, CA: Hay House, 2004.

Jay, Francine. *Miss Minimalist: Inspiration to Downsize, Declutter, and Simplify*. Medford, NJ: Anja Press, 2011.

Johnston, Russell Gerald. *Random Wisdom*. Bloomington, IN: iUniverse, 2009.

Kennedy, David Daniel. *Feng Shui for Dummies*. Hoboken, NJ: Wiley, 2001.

Kent, Tami Lynn. *Wild Feminine: Finding Power, Spirit, and Joy in the Female Body*. New York: Atria, 2011.

Kidman, Diane. *Beauty Gone Wild! Herbal Recipes for Gorgeous Skin and Hair*. Carp(e) Libris, 2012.

Kingston, Karen. *Clear Your Clutter with Feng Shui*. New York: Broadway, 1999.

Lau, Theodora. *The Handbook of Chinese Horoscopes*. New York: HarperCollins, 1979.

Linn, Denise. *Secrets and Mysteries: The Glory and Pleasure of Being a Woman*. Carlsbad, CA: Hay House, 2002.

Listfield, Emily. "Beauty: What's Age Got to Do with It?" *More Magazine*. December 2012, 46–52.

Llewellyn. *Llewellyn's Magical Almanac*. Woodbury, MN: Llewellyn, yearly.

Lustig, Andrea Pomeranz. *How to Look Expensive: A Beauty Editor's Secrets to Getting Gorgeous without Breaking the Bank*. New York: Penguin, 2012.

Maggiore, Evana. *Fashion Feng Shui: The Power of Dressing with Intention*. Winchester, MA: Mansion, 2007.

Medici, Marina. *Good Magic*. New York: Fireside, 1998.

Melody. *Love Is In the Earth: A Kaleidoscope of Crystals*. Wheat Ridge, CO: Earth Love Publishing House, 1995.

Miller, Richard Alan, and Iona Miller. *The Magical and Ritual Use of Perfumes*. Rochester, VT: Destiny Books, 1990.

Mojay, Gabriel. *Aromatherapy for Healing the Spirit: Restoring Emotional and Mental Balance with Essential Oils*. Rochester, VT: Healing Arts, 1997.

Moorey, Teresa. *The Fairy Bible: The Definitive Guide to the World of Fairies*. New York: Sterling, 2008.

Nozedar, Adele. *The Element Encyclopedia of Secret Signs and Symbols: The Ultimate A–Z Guide from Alchemy to the Zodiac*. London: Harper Element, 2007.

Oliver, Vicky. *The Millionaire's Handbook: How to Look and Act Like a Millionaire Even if You're Not*. New York: Skyhorse, 2011.

Pierson, P. J., and Mary Shipley. *Aromatherapy for Everyone: Discover the Scents of Health and Happiness with Essential Oils*. Garden City Park, NY: Square One, 2004.

Robin, Jennifer. *Growing More Beautiful: An Artful Approach to Personal Style*. Petaluma, CA: Artful Press, 2008.

Rose, Jeanne. *Jeanne Rose's Herbal Body Book: The Herbal Way to Natural Beauty and Health for Men and Women*. New York: Grosset & Dunlap, 1976.

Savacool, Julia. "Where Age Is No Object." *More Magazine*. December 2012, 92–99.

Sexton, Anne. *The Complete Poems*. New York: Houghton Miffin, 1981.

Shinn, Florence Scovel. *The Wisdom of Florence Scovel Shinn*. New York: Fireside, 1989.

Snyder, Kimberly. *The Beauty Detox Solution: Eat Your Way to Beautiful Skin, Renewed Energy, and the Body You've Always Wanted*. Buffalo, NY: Harlequin, 2011.

Vreeland, Diana. *D.V.* Cambridge, MS: De Capo Press, 1984.

Webster, Richard. *Face Reading Quick and Easy*. Woodbury, MN: Llewellyn, 2012.

———. *Pendulum Magic for Beginners: Tap Into Your Inner Wisdom*. Woodbury, MN: Llewellyn, 2012.

White, Suzanne. *The New Chinese Astrology*. New York: St. Martin's Press, 1993.

Whitehurst, Tess. *The Good Energy Book: Creating Harmony and Balance for Yourself and Your Home*. Woodbury, MN: Llewellyn, 2012.

———. *The Magic of Flowers: A Guide to Their Metaphysical Uses & Properties*. Woodbury, MN: Llewellyn, 2013.

———. *Magical Clutter Clearing Boot Camp*. Venice, CA: Tess Whitehurst, 2011.

———. *Magical Housekeeping: Simple Charms and Practical Tips for Creating a Harmonious Home*. Woodbury, MN: Llewellyn, 2010.

Wiseman, Sara. *The Four Passages of the Heart: 365 Daily Illuminations to Transform Your Life*. Bedford, IN: NorLightsPress, 2012.

Wolfe, Amber. *Personal Alchemy: A Handbook of Healing and Transformation*. St. Paul, MN: Llewellyn, 1993.

Woolfolk, Joanna Martine. *The Only Astrology Book You'll Ever Need*. New York: Madison, 1982.

Film and Television

Bill Cunningham New York. Richard Press. First Thought, 2010.

Diana Vreeland: The Eye Has to Travel. Lisa Immordino Vreeland. Gloss Studio, 2011.

It. Clarence C. Badger. Paramount, 1927.

Lagerfeld Confidential. Rodolphe Marconi. Backup Films/ Realitism, 2007.

"Lucy Gets a Paris Gown." *I Love Lucy*. CBS. 19 March 1956.

Unzipped. Douglass Keeve. Miramax, 1995.

What the Bleep Do We Know? William Arntz, Betsy Chasse, Mark Vicente. Roadside Attractions, 2004.

Websites

Lunarium.co.uk

TheSartorialist.com

ACKNOWLEDGMENTS

I would like to thank all the authors and experts whom I quoted and from whom I drew inspiration. Many thanks also to Amy Glaser, Elysia Gallo, Becky Zins, Bill Krause, Sandra Weschcke, Kat Sanborn, Ellen Lawson, Anna Levine, Bethany Onsgard, Sally Heuer, and everyone at Llewellyn. Further gratitude to Ted Bruner, Brandi Palecheck, Annie Wilder, Ellen Dugan, Mayumin Hosoya, Erin Amabile, Rachel Avalon, Janine Jordan, Emily Whitehurst, Sedona Soulfire, Angela Taylor, Tara Amabile, Aron Whitehurst, Joel Whitehurst, Courtney Lichtermann, Jonathan Kirsch, and the lovely woman I sat next to on the flight back from Denver.

This book is lovingly dedicated to my late grandmother (and fashion angel!) Cecelia Whitehurst.

To order, call 1-877-NEW-WRLD

Prices subject to change without notice

Order at llewellyn.com 24 hours a day, 7 days a week!

Magical Housekeeping

*Simple Charms & Practical Tips for Creating a
Harmonious Home*

Tess Whitehurst

Every inch and component of your home is filled with an invisible life force and unique magical energy. *Magical Housekeeping* teaches readers how to sense, change, channel, and direct these energies to create harmony in their homes, joy in their hearts, and success in all areas of their lives.

In this engaging guide, energy consultant and teacher Tess Whitehurst shares her secrets for creating an energetically powerful and positive home. Written for those new to metaphysics as well as experienced magical practitioners, *Magical Housekeeping* will teach readers how to summon success, happiness, romance, abundance, and all the desires of the heart. And, by guiding them to make changes in both the seen and unseen worlds simultaneously, this dynamic and delightful book will help to activate and enhance readers' intuition and innate magical power.

978-0-7387-1985-6
$5^3/_{16}$ x 8 • 240 pp. • $16.95

To order, call 1-877-NEW-WRLD

Prices subject to change without notice

Order at llewellyn.com 24 hours a day, 7 days a week!

The Good Energy Book

*Creating Harmony and Balance for Yourself
and Your Home*

Tess Whitehurst

This gem of a book teaches you how to become a fountain of good energy. Discover how to maintain positive energy in your home—and establish lifelong habits and perspectives that will bring happiness and attract all good things.

Popular author and columnist Tess Whitehurst presents a holistic system for keeping your energy positive and traversing any place, situation, or challenge with confidence, clarity, and grace. She shares fun and effective techniques that draw from both the physical and energetic realms, telling you not just what to do, but also why you're doing it and even how it works.

978-0-7387-2772-1
$5^3/_{16}$ x 8 • 240 pp. • $14.95

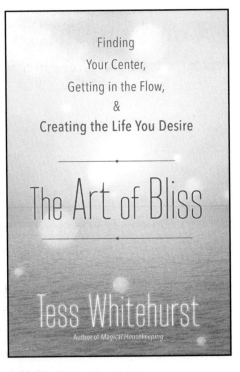

Finding
Your Center,
Getting in the Flow,
&
Creating the Life You Desire

The Art of Bliss

Tess Whitehurst

Author of *Magical Housekeeping*

To order, call 1-877-NEW-WRLD

Prices subject to change without notice

Order at llewellyn.com 24 hours a day, 7 days a week!

The Art of Bliss

Finding Your Center, Getting in the Flow,
and Creating the Life You Desire

Tess Whitehurst

Bring harmony and balance to every area of your life with this gentle and loving guide to beautiful living and personal evolution.

Popular author Tess Whitehurst offers a unique and fun magical system for reconnecting with your bliss, also known as your innate life force energy. Weaving together the I Ching, feng shui, and a sprinkling of magic, she teaches you to activate your nine life keys for success and happiness. Become attuned to the areas of serenity, life path, synchronicity, creativity, romance, radiance, prosperity, harmony, and synergy—and awaken each with affirmations, breathwork, prayer, meditation, smudging, rituals, and many more energetically potent tools.

978-0-7387-3196-4
$5^3/_{16}$ x 8 • 312 pp. • $16.99

To Write to the Author

If you wish to contact the author or would like more information about this book, please write to the author in care of Llewellyn Worldwide and we will forward your request. Both the author and the publisher appreciate hearing from you and learning of your enjoyment of this book and how it has helped you. Llewellyn Worldwide cannot guarantee that every letter written to the author can be answered, but all will be forwarded. Please write to:

Tess Whitehurst
Llewellyn Worldwide
2143 Wooddale Drive
Woodbury, MN 55125-2989

Please enclose a self-addressed stamped envelope for reply
or $1.00 to cover costs. If outside the USA, enclose
an international postal reply coupon.

Many of Llewellyn's authors have websites with additional information and resources. For more information, please visit our website:

WWW.LLEWELLYN.COM